SHAKESPEARE AND THE ACTORS

SHAKESPEARE
AND THE ACTORS

❧

IVOR BROWN

THE BODLEY HEAD
LONDON   SYDNEY
TORONTO

© Ivor Brown 1970
SBN 370 01324 7
Printed and bound in Great Britain for
The Bodley Head Ltd
9 Bow Street, London w c 2
by William Clowes & Sons Ltd
London and Beccles
Set in Monotype Garamond
First published 1970

Contents

List of Illustrations

❧❧❧

CHAPTER I

Men of Parts

❦

THE COPIOUS flow of books about Shakespeare comes mainly from the Universities. Since there has recently been a large increase in the number of Universities the stream grows wider and more rapid. The new trend is inevitably towards concentration upon science and technology. It is said that the man or woman with an 'Arts' degree finds further employment harder to find except in becoming an 'Arts' teacher. However that may be the Arts are still given their Chairs. The Professors of English Literature become more numerous and, to judge by their lectures reprinted in books, there is a broader and more imaginative approach to Shakespeare than was made by some of their predecessors. The new Universities have stages on which plays are acted as well as daises on which lectures are given. In schools, too, there is far more understanding that plays are things to be acted and that a text written for the theatre differs from a book written to be read.

In my boyhood I was put to *The Tempest* amid the ill-tempered yawns and groans of a master who had not the slightest understanding of poetry or the theatre. He respected propriety and, to avoid a vulgar giggle, insisted that 'horse-piss' should be amended in our reading to 'horse-pond'. Of *The Merchant of Venice*, inevitable task, he cared chiefly that we should be able to explain what the Rialto was. He obviously loathed Shakespeare as he, more justifiably, loathed the young louts sitting at his feet which had once been nimble enough to win high honours on cricket grounds and football fields. So had he qualified to be our guide to Parnassus.

The change has been excellent and I would like to think that Shakespeare has escaped entirely from the academic and scholastic

9

dominion of the person whom Frank Harris repeatedly described as Dry-as-dust. The conception of Shakespeare as a play-house professional and a harassed human being with his private heart-aches and his public chores has been gradually admitted by the more sensible and sensitive exponents of 'Eng Lit'. The rescuers have done for the Bard what Gilbert Murray did for the Greek drama. That subject was made insufferable to me at school because I had to spend my time in extracting what meaning I could from the tangled choruses and the 'variant readings' of the pedantic editors. At Oxford, with Murray lecturing or talking in a friendly seminar at his home, the clouds lifted, the light broke in, and one seemed to be sitting in the Athenian sunlight in one of their rock-cut theatres. Education still wedges Shakespeare irremovably into the 'set subjects' and while he is there he must suffer from misunderstanding and dislike unless the teachers, at whatever level, have the quickening quality which raises instruction to illumination.

But there is still one aspect of Shakespeare that is frequently overlooked in the comment on his plays. It is too often assumed that the text is exactly as he wrote it, a considered literary product. But the words were not an end-product. They were the flexible material of a theatrical effect, written by an actor for actors. That material was subject to cutting and reshaping in discussion before rehearsal or during the preparation of a production. The players were the partners not the employees of the author. His script was to be brought to life by the personal magnetism and professional skill of those who were to animate the characters. If they had their opinions of what could best be done with a speech or a scene they could say so.

The deliberate writing of a play had come late into the theatre from the streets and the platforms where improvised mummery had been fertile. When Shakespeare became a dramatist the age-long game of 'Let's Pretend' had become formalised by the actors' preference for written scripts and the ability of the poets and wits to produce them. The antics had become an art, but few of the writers for the stage (Ben Jonson was a notable exception) saw themselves as contributors to the high dignity of literature with an expectation of respect and survival for every word written for the players. (Epics and Sonnets were another matter.)

They were often players themselves with a team to serve. They might be lucky, as Shakespeare was, in the ability of their colleagues to be worthy of the glorious words set down for them and so enthral the public. The players might think some of their appointed speeches inadequate and drop or amend them. That was especially true of the comedians convinced that this was sorry stuff for a clown and inserting their own notion of a livelier joke. Against that Shakespeare protested and Kempe left the company, probably in resentment. One can imagine him remarking as he walked out that he had got more laughs with his invented drollery than his author had got with his script. Before Shakespeare made Hamlet protest against gagging he may have been provoked by the occasional discovery that the audience was in fact more amused by the antic jester than by the authorised jest. It is worth noting that while he grumbled about gagging he advised cutting. When Polonius complained about the length of the First Player's specimen speech Hamlet immediately decided that its length should be cut. For him there was nothing sacrosanct about a speech if it was windy and boring. In the first case Hamlet spoke as an author, in the second as an actor who knew what would damage a play and behaved as an editor while he was engaged as an interpreter.

Shakespeare had begun as an actor towards the end of the fifteen-eighties and he stayed an actor at least until 1603. There is no evidence that he continued after that and none that he stopped acting then. By that time he was a major playwright with a steady output. Output may seem a crude word to apply to the work of a genius. But it describes his ready provision of acting material and his willingness to help other writers, as he did, probably, in *Timon of Athens* and certainly in *Pericles*. That he contributed to *The Two Noble Kinsmen* by John Fletcher is now widely accepted because passages of typically Shakespearian style are included. The actors must be served and he did not disdain to aid the weaker hands. He was ready to do some patching up.

More important financially was his position as an Actor-Sharer and a House-Sharer. In the former category he was responsible for finding and casting plays. In the latter he shared the cares of finding and maintaining theatrical premises. It was burdensome, but here lay the possibility of financial security since the King's Men were popular and prosperous. To have had the best poet and playwright would not have advanced them in royal and general favour if they had not had the best actors or at least actors who could make the most of the scripts provided. It is hard to imagine Shakespeare starting on a play without the cast and its theatrical possibilities in mind. His work has kept its compelling power undiminished and even increasing because he could feel the parts with an actor's intuition. In the jargon of today he 'identified'. There has been constant analysis of his characters and their psychology as though they were people in books, but their creator was devising them with an immediate purpose in mind. They were to be seen in the flesh and heard by an audience. They must grip.

As to the money involved we know only that the dramatists and minor actors were poorly paid. A play of five acts was sold outright for five or six pounds. The fee for amending old plays for revival was two or three pounds. This is revealed in the note-books of Henslowe who grew rich on the profits of Paris Garden where bulls and bears were baited as well as on the takings in a theatre. There were plenty of volunteers for jobs as playwrights and players; exploitation was easy. The players of 'bit' parts, known as Hired Men, were obtainable at ten shillings a week. The earnings of an established and popular player depended on his position as a Sharer and the amount to be shared. Shakespeare's income came from that source. He had been a Sharer since 1594. If he played a part himself after that it was not for the pay. The company was flourishing and the money coming in. That he could buy the 'Great House', New Place, in Stratford in 1598 was due to his membership of what Hamlet called 'a fellowship of players'. His fellows owed much to him for writing superb roles. His debt to them for excellent performance he well knew. The title of 'fellowship' was earned on both sides.

He need not have continued to be an actor, working in a profession which, on the evidence of the Sonnets, he sometimes believed to 'brand' him in a humiliating way. There was a reason for that. Actors were nobodies only permitted to work at their craft if protected by a Somebody. That was a galling thought but there is no need to see this sense of grievance as an enduring rancour. The Sonnets were not written for publication and general reading. They were offered to a man of title by one who was his social inferior. The idea that he was a poet of quality had been suggested to him by the success of *Venus and Adonis* and *Lucrece*. But he did not persevere in that line. There was a limited future in that. He had found his proper and his profitable sphere. The 'brand' was not a lasting wound. He had talked in the Sonnets not only of frustration but of living 'on top of happy hours'. The abiding happiness came in the heat and dust of the theatre, in the excitement of exciting an audience, and in being an actor himself while serving other actors in a way beyond the power of any rival dramatist.

His pen was unquenchable. His plays were in great demand and usually pleased the Court and the public. He could have let the acting go, but he did not. There he was, finding time to study a long part in two of Ben Jonson's plays in 1598 and 1603, and probably small ones in his own. He was memorising, rehearsing, and performing at a time when he was most busily and triumphantly engaged as a dramatist. This side of Shakespeare's career receives far less attention than it should. It fascinates me who for most of my life have been in and out of theatres as a dramatic critic and later on talking to actors and hearing their troubles. My wife has been a director of important London productions and from her, too, I know the constant trials and sometimes the turmoil of casting and producing a play and coping with nervous, sensitive, and difficult people exposed to the hazards of public failure amid the hopes of a rewarding success. It is unfair to the theatre people of today, in whatever capacity they are working, that Shakespeare, the dedicated actor, should be so much forgotten while the tributes to Shakespeare the writer are as unstinted and incessant as they are deserved.

We lack the evidence which would tell us 'the inside story' of a new production by Shakespeare. Nearly every play which reaches London nowadays has had a secret history of doubts and delays; it has been wrangled over and partially rewritten. Any theatrical enterprise is a co-operative enterprise; it may justify the description of a creative partnership. But often it is carried on by temperamental and jealous people who are of all persons the least inclined to co-operate. We are probably wrong to visualise the Chamberlain's and the King's Men as tetchy and fractious. They did not split up and scatter. They were remarkably cohesive while there were quarrels, partings, and failures in other companies. Kempe, who was a Sharer and one of the leaders in 1594, did go and so did some lesser men. But with the other senior partners it was death not division that interrupted their excellent alliance.

If plague did not invade the city and close the theatres altogether they were kept constantly at work. There were disastrous epidemics in 1593, 1603, and 1609, interrupting three phases of Shakespeare's career. At the best of times the players had no hope of long runs which would allow them to settle down. They formed what we would call a repertory team, constantly renewing and reviving their successes while they were seeking to find a new one. It is unlikely that they were under as hard a pressure as were the employees of Henslowe whose luckily preserved Diary shows him to have been a Gradgrind of his age and its Show Business. He made loans to his needy script-writers. He regarded them contemptuously as drudges desperate for cash in hand and in this way he bound them to his service. 'Should these fellows', he wrote, 'come out of my debt I shall have no rule over them.' His hired dramatists and players were on a treadmill. In a year and a quarter they provided and performed fifty-five new or newly revived plays. There was quantity indeed and quality of poetry sometimes. Amid so much bustle performance must frequently

have been ragged. The lack of settled conditions and of the ability
to take time over a production challenged the authors and actors
to make up with their words and their voices for the impoverished
and hustled presentation.

There have been various categories of theatre down the
centuries. During the eighteenth and most of the nineteenth
century the great actor was sovereign. He drew the crowds. A
Shakespeare play was regarded by the critics and connoisseurs as
a medium for display of histrionic quality. During the last quarter
of the nineteenth century the author began to assert himself as a
man with a message. After him came the producer, now called
the director, the man with a method. These three aspects of power
and prominence were typified by Irving as the dynamic player,
by Shaw (following Ibsen) as the dynamo of the theatre of ideas,
and by Reinhardt in Europe, Stanislavsky in Russia and Granville-
Barker in England as men who applied new methods, the first
to spectacle and the two latter to faithful interpretation of the
playwright's purpose. In Shakespeare's time and company there
was a shifting balance of power. The hacks who had slaved for
Henslowe were replaced by the playwright who, at least in
Shakespeare's case, had status and authority equal to that of
Burbage, since both were Sharers as well as supreme in their own
spheres.

When the Chamberlain's Men had been established in royal
favour in 1594 and proceeded to win public favour also there
was no necessity to drive ahead at Henslowe's furious pace. But
they had to 'plod on and keep the passion fresh'. It has been plausibly calculated that they were in the habit of presenting fifteen
plays in a year if there was no hampering epidemic. Shakespeare
was contributing one or sometimes two of these; between 1596
and 1600 he may even have completed three in a year while he
may also have been acting in some of them. These were not our
little three-act comedies with a flimsy plot sufficient for one act
and needing only a small cast. His plays with their five acts, their
battles and crowds and rhetoric were three-dimensional, long,
broad, and sometimes deep, giants by our standards. Even if this

assessment of the numbers staged be wrong there can be no doubt about the cares of responsibility overhanging the heads of the Sharers. There was always the question of 'What next and how to do it?' Who shall play what? Will Burbage like the principal role? Are enough Hired Men available and reliable? Is there a boy of sufficient experience to be trusted with a Juliet or a Cleopatra?

What happened when Shakespeare came in with a new script? He knew intimately from his daily contacts the proclivities and capacities of his colleagues. Partly he wrote as his genius moved him after discovering a suitable subject, partly as one who had to provide the right role for the right man or promising boy as well as the right play to fill the theatre. He must have had a talk with the other Sharers about the new topic in his mind. When they had realised his value they would have been fools to raise difficulties. So he had gone to his desk with the actors foremost in his mind.

He emerged with a product which, whatever its other merits, had to be legible. That was an important consideration then. The labour of making copies by hand added to the delay and cost of a production. A trifling expense, it may be thought, but in Shakespeare's workshop the small amounts had to be carefully counted. There was the galling contrast of the lavish spending on the revels of the exhibitionist nobility at Court; as much as two thousand pounds was spent on the sumptuous mounting of a Court Masque for its frisking amateurs. The professionals in the play-house received ten or possibly twenty pounds for a Command Performance according to the amount of travel involved.

They might get an occasional bonus payment which came as a welcome gift. They had no steady subsidy on which to rely. The men of title who gave their names and protection to those who would otherwise have been rogues and vagabonds, liable to public flogging, were essential champions, but they did not guarantee production costs and salaries. The plays had to pay their way or the players were out of work and out of what money they expected. Those who now use the term 'commercial theatre' with contempt should remember that Shakespeare was one of its dutiful and diligent servants. The players could not look to a benign Arts Council for a vast benefaction and think themselves harshly used by a Philistine society if they did not get it.

Without being unduly fanciful one can imagine Shakespeare arriving for a first rehearsal. We have sufficient evidence about the equipment and conditions to avoid complete guesswork. He has his own manuscript. All such holographs were known as 'foul papers'. (That his handiwork was the reverse of a mess was attested by Heminge and Condell when they told the readers of the Folio that they had 'scarce received from him a blot in his papers'.) Others may have produced a text so blotched and scribbled over with alterations that they were cursed as botchers by those who had hurriedly to decipher their words before memorising them. There was also a Fair Copy made by the company's Book-Keeper who combined the roles of scrivener and prompter and sometimes, it seems, of stage-manager as well.

One in that position can, if competent, contribute much to a success or, if he is a muddler, involve author and actors in an unmerited disaster. Stage-managers, however efficient, are never mentioned in dramatic criticism. Their names are to be discovered in small print. How many who buy a programme notice or remember them? Directors have so far asserted themselves that some of them may now get more attention than any other of the parties in the production. But they depend on the vigilance and promptness of level-headed stage-managers. Shakespeare must have known that. He may have been one himself as he made his strenuous way up the ladder of his career.

The Book-Keeper had made, or had ordered a scrivener to make, the Fair Copy. This had been sent to the Master of the Revels for 'allowance'. There was a strict censorship of plays, mainly for political reasons. There must be no incitements to rebellion in the events portrayed and no recognisable denigration of the people in authority. Shakespeare had learned his lesson when the spectacle of a king dethroned in *Richard II* had involved his company in trouble with a Queen whose own sovereignty was shortly to be challenged. After that there was no suspicion of disloyalty and the Fair Copies passed the official inspection. The Court's chosen were not looking for disgrace and dismissal. When the Fair Copies returned they were the property of the company and jealously guarded.

One or two replicas had to be made, for safety's sake, but that safety measure had its risks. Some printers were pirates, ready for a grab if a text had the sweet smell of a play-house success in the air and so could be profitable in Fleet Street and Little Britain where the bookmen clustered. The rival acting companies were also eager to purloin a valuable script. An extra and complete copy of a play was coveted by the player of a leading role who could thus study it properly. The lesser men received their parts in scrappy excerpts. Could Burbage be satisfied with the enormous part of Hamlet supplied to him as a sheaf of tiny slips of paper? For the general guidance of the company there was the Plot, a concise account in large letters of the action, the various scenes, and the participating characters. Specimens of these have survived. The Book-Keeper made them, presumably with the dramatist's supervision. They were pasted up on a board in the theatre for the information and briefing of the team about their entrances and exits.

Thus, with an anxious group crowding round the rudimentary Plot and with their bits of paper in hand, the team assembled to grapple with a new play by Shakespeare. He may have read all or most of it through for their instruction. It is most unlikely that he gave his company a lecture in the modern manner on the psychology of the characters and the symbolism inherent in the treatment of his theme. They were there to put on a show and please the public and that quickly. If the author's subconscious self had been at work on the 'thoughts that lie beyond the reaches of our souls' and had coloured his language and his imagery accordingly that was his business. One can see a bewildered player muttering to himself, 'What the devil does all this stuff mean?', but not saying as much to the author. They had only a week or two. The play must be ready.

Somebody had to be in charge, arranging the moves, regulating

the pace, selecting the points to be made and the lines to stress.
The dramatist and pamphleteer Dekker mentioned a 'guider'.
Who guided at the Globe? It could have been the leading player
whose position Burbage held continuously while Shakespeare
was his fellow-Sharer.

Up to his death in 1917 Sir Herbert Beerbohm Tree found time
and energy to be at once producer and protagonist. He needed
and had beside him a stage-manager with directive as well as
organising ability. The system encouraged egoism in the dominating taker of star parts. But the public did not resent it and the
other actors took it as part of the routine. Their turn might come.
The audience then was much more attracted by the magnetic and
almost mesmeric figure of an unquestionable star than by the
text of Shakespeare which gave him his strutting-ground. Burbage may have felt that he was the real magician who filled the
house, but, if Shakespeare ever was piqued by this, he did not
sulk, quarrel and take his scripts elsewhere.

Theatrical egoism can fairly be censured if it interferes with
the purpose of a serious playwright and distorts the balance of his
work. But it need not worry the ordinary dramatist who has a
living to earn by neat contrivance of a conventional story for the
stage and naturally wants it to attract large audiences and bring in
good royalty payments. Shaw, while denouncing the selfish
treatment of a text simply for the leading player's glorification,
frankly admitted that the London theatre of the eighteen-nineties,
while he was a dramatic critic, would be bankrupt without the
personal appeal of the star. He himself would go his own way as
a playwright and refused to his cost to serve his market, but he
realised that others could not afford to do so and he did not blame
them if they wrote to suit the prevailing system.

The great Knights of the Victorian and Edwardian theatre
added confidence to capacity. The bestowal of their titles proved
that a new status had been given to a profession once supposed
to be disreputable. Theirs was no longer a 'branded' name.
Shakespeare and his colleagues, even more favoured by King
James than by Queen Elizabeth, helped in their time the upward

move in social ranking. It would not be held that a Groom of the Royal Chamber, with a special robe for a Coronation march, was still a rogue and vagabond.

The tide of comment turned against the imperious actor-managers who did not require a third party to teach them their business. But their individualism became a target for the new critical marksmanship. They were reasonably accused of crowding Shakespeare out of his own plays with their vast spread of canvas and elaborate spectacular effects. For these Shakespeare's Globe and the Command Performances on improvised stages at Court or in noblemen's houses provided no opportunity or temptation. His lines could not be buried in a military panorama which, on the evidence of the Prologues in *Henry V*, he would have liked to include. The simplicity of production in his time annoyed him as a frustrated showman, as those Prologues candidly stated, but protected him from seeing his text overlaid by pageantry.

The actor-managers who submerged the stage in massive spectacle were also charged with mauling the text to suit their own parts. The attack was intensified by other critics after Shaw had courageously hammered Irving, which was a form of blasphemy to the faithful public of the Lyceum Theatre. If Shaw had continued as a critic when Tree and his scene-painters were presenting Shakespeare in sumptuous trappings there would have been further vehement assault on established reputations. But improvement came. It could be said that Shakespeare was set free.

In Granville-Barker's productions there was scrupulous regard for the text. The words were not trimmed, but the settings were. His ideas and techniques, which delighted a minority, were too far ahead of their time to be profitable at the box-office. He did not dispense altogether with scenery; he diminished and refined it with an elegance that was then thought austere by those accustomed to spectacle and deprived by its absence. He made the most of the words while he charmed the discerning eye with the neat economy of his settings. He combated the idea that Shakespeare would be dull unless dolled up. He was never drab as William Poel was ready to be. Working with no money and in what premises he could get, he used a completely bare stage. As to scenery he was a Nudist. This was not being true to Shakespeare who would have welcomed some degree of eye-capturing showmanship and did write for it in his later plays, especially in his last, *Henry VIII*. When Masques had become fashionable he could suit the fashion as far as the resources of his theatre allowed. Ben Jonson, as a classicist and proud of it, was doctrinaire. Shakespeare was practical and versatile, always a completely involved man of the theatre.

Poel insisted that the words must be delivered without cutting and in full. But he made one exception. He was a purist, as we say, in his attitude to the text, but he was also a Puritan in taste and was ready to cut what offended his sense of propriety. Then economic pressure came in to assist his anti-spectacular school of thought. It had been possible for Irving and Tree to mount a vast Shakespearian production and withdraw it after three months to launch another, possibly with a profit already made, and certainly without serious financial discouragement if the theatre had been well filled during a run which seems short to us. Then the cost of labour and materials, which had been astonishingly cheap, began to rise steadily. There could be no more acres of canvas and fortunately no more of the numerous and time-wasting changes of scene. Grandeur was doomed. Even if the public still wanted it they could not have it. In our time any large Shakespearian production must have substantial subsidy and even so the spectacular side, ingenious in its economy, is meagre by the old standard.

For Shakespeare and Burbage there was no thought of a dominating third party. They must have had their specialist who excelled in the staging of a bout of fencing or in the contrivance of such magical spectacle as was possible on their stage. If the Book-Keeper with his prompting to do was also the stage-manager he needed assistants to see that the much-used trapdoor worked efficiently and that the miraculous effects required were forthcoming. In *The Tempest* (III, iii) there is this stage direction: 'Thunder and lightning. Enter Ariel as a harpy; claps his wings on the table; and, with a quaint device, the banquet vanishes.' A harpy is a bird with a woman's body. So the boy-player cast as Ariel flew in. Lowering with a winch became a familiar exercise. The quaint device must have been a trapdoor effect. The banquet had been brought in by 'several strange Shapes' with 'Prospero invisible above', who was presumably speaking from some niche in the roof, known as 'the heavens'.

For Shakespearian productions at the roofed-in Blackfriars Theatre, taken over in 1608, the use of the winch for air-borne actors was easier to work from the ceiling. In *Cymbeline* (V, iv), 'Jupiter descends in thunder and lightning, sitting upon an eagle; he throws a thunderbolt.' The Hired Man must have prayed not to be thrown from his mount; as he launched his missile he had to depend for his safety on the efficacy of the winch and its operators. The organisation involved, more and more necessary as 'quaint devices' were more used, was intricate and exacting. Whoever took charge of the direction, author or actor, required his technicians. The Hired Men had to be handy-men. When Shakespeare had retired to Stratford the scripts, as Granville-Barker pointed out, were delivered to the company with an increased insertion of stage-directions. This suggests that before this he had been a guider on the spot and, when away, put more of his guidance in writing because he would not be there to give it verbally and look to the execution.

So one can visualise without straining probability the man who enjoyed acting sitting in self-denial with his manuscript in hand through most of the rehearsals. There need be no guesswork in our ideas of what he wanted. Hamlet's speeches to the players are explicit. They are irrelevant to the play and may have been cut in performance unless they were regarded as a slap at rival companies and a tart criticism which many of the audience would appreciate. There was carelessness in the insertion of these passages. Shakespeare complained about clowns interrupting 'some necessary question of the play' while he was doing exactly that. The performance of *The Murder of Gonzago* was essential to the exposure of Claudius. 'Talking shop' about the misbehaviour of

comedians was not. But this bubbled up when he saw a chance to
voice a fair complaint. Kempe's clowning, once so valuable,
had become a nuisance. There had been a row and a parting.
Here was an answer to those members of the public who had
relished and now missed Kempe's drolleries and thought he had
been unjustly victimised.

The instruction was that of one demanding realism in performance even though many of his plots were as fanciful as could
be. Credibility in a story did not appeal to the Elizabethans. Our
kind of complaint, which seizes on unlikely or implausible events
and holds them to be fatal faults in the plot and motivation of a
play, was then far from any play-goer's mind. It is obvious that
the public would swallow any pretence, notably the fictions that
all girls are the same in the dark and that characters will not be
recognised by their dearest friends if they change their clothes.
Under compulsion of the players anything would be believed if
there were power in the tragedy, gaiety in the comedy, and music
in the words. Yet Shakespeare demanded that the acting should be
natural, however fantastic the events. The pompous formalism of
the histrionic method which prevailed when he joined the
profession vexed him. As a 'guider' he would cut out the routine
flourish of the arms which sawed the air. The gait too must be
normal with the familiar strutting abandoned. He knew all the
face-pulling tricks. Says Buckingham in *Richard III* (III, v):

> *True, I can counterfeit the deep tragedian,*
> *Speak and look back and pry on every side,*
> *Tremble and start at wagging of a straw,*
> *Intending deep suspicion; ghastly looks*
> *Are at my service, like enforced smiles.*

Shakespeare did not desire a tame performance and the show of
'flat, unraised spirits' mentioned in *Henry V*. Animation there
must be, but exaggeration he would not have. Passionate scenes
were to be made persuasive by the art of 'the well-graced actor',
not ruined by rant and roaring. It is inconceivable that he would
have tolerated the inaudibility which has been the curse of modern

acting in the theatre where there is no television knob to turn for increasing the sound. He did not write lines to be 'thrown away', a form of waste which is so stupidly thought to create natural speech. A theatre is an unnatural place and demands acceptance of the fact. While he denounced the ear-splitting mouthing of the town-crier style and asked for delivery of his words 'trippingly on the tongue' they must not be lost in a gallop of utterance. Hamlet admirably as well as angrily prescribed the rules of speech. We are left in no doubt as to the advice that Shakespeare gave at rehearsals. He had been put through the bad, old ways in the years before he joined the Chamberlain's Men; he spoke with an actor's experience of all schools when, having won a position of authority, he demanded new and better methods and evidently carried his company with him. If they neglected his counsel to the extent of enraging him he could afford to take his pen to another stall in the market.

CHAPTER II

Shakespeare and his Quality

❧

'THIS WILLIAM, being naturally inclined to poetry and acting, . . . was an actor at one of the play-houses and did act exceeding well.' Thus wrote John Aubrey in his fragmentary but useful notes on Shakespeare in his *Brief Lives*. The statement is positive and the compliment is unqualified. Previously included are pieces of information which are qualified.

'His father was a butcher, and I have been told heretofore by some of the neighbours, that when he was a boy he exercised his father's trade, but when he kill'd a calfe he would doe it in a high style, and make a speech. There was at that time another butcher's son in this towne that was held not at all inferior to him for a naturall witt, his acquaintance and coetanean, but dyed young.'

John Shakespeare, the poet's father, dealt in wool and leather goods, especially gloves, and may have added slaughtering to his salesmanship. That the boy added drama and oratory to the repulsive killing is unlikely if we judge by the humanitarian opinions later expressed. In *Henry VI, Part II* (III, i) Henry's pity for the doomed Duke of Gloucester evokes this memory of a Stratford childhood.

> *And as the butcher takes away the calf,*
> *And binds the wretch, and beats it when it strays,*
> *Bearing it to the bloody slaughter-house;*
> *Even so, remorseless, have they borne him hence:*
> *And as the dam runs lowing up and down,*
> *Looking the way her harmless young one went,*
> *And can do naught but wail her darling's loss;*
> *Even so myself bewails good Gloster's case*
> *With sad unhelpful tears . . .*

This certainly does not suggest gleeful play-acting amid the gore. Of that Aubrey, who wrote a hundred years after Shakespeare's boyhood, only said that he had been told of it by some of his father's neighbours. Such old tittle-tattle need not be taken as evidence but it is quite likely that the young William enjoyed dramatising less gory events and spouting in 'a high style' with a like-minded companion.

Aubrey also said that Shakespeare 'came to London at eighteen' in order to be an actor and to this he added 'I guesse'. If the guess is correct the young husband had fled from his wife with exceptional speed. Shakespeare was born in April, 1564, and married in November, 1582. His eldest child, Susanna, was born in May, 1583. If he 'came to London' before he was nineteen he had not even waited for the arrival of his first-born. The marriage may have begun unhappily, but such a swift callous desertion is hardly credible. Aubrey, often a reckless recorder of gossip, did not report it with any confidence. But he had no hesitation about the claim that, when he had become established as a player, Shakespeare acted 'exceedingly well'. To this he added in a bracket that Ben Jonson 'was never a good actor but an excellent instructor'. What was his authority for this assured information about the London play-houses?

One of his informants about the theatre was the actor 'Old Mr Beeston' whom Dryden called 'the chronicle of the stage'. He died in 1682. Another was 'Mr Lacy, the player'. Lacy was a dancing-master who fought in the Royalist army during the civil war, took to acting with Killigrew's company after the Restoration, and was reputed to be the favourite comedian of King Charles II. Pepys recounted that Lacy appeared in 'the best part' in *The Taming of the Shrew* which the diarist found 'but a mean play'. He was not impressed by the acting, 'by reason of the words, I suppose, not being understood by me'. We need not be prejudiced against Lacy by that remark. Pepys may have been a little fuddled and he sometimes confessed to being more attracted by women in the audience than by men on the stage. It was probably not Shakespeare's own play but Lacy's adaptation of

The Taming of the Shrew that Pepys saw, misunderstood and disliked.

For Pepys and Aubrey to hear the talk of these players was to be in touch with the vanished conditions in which Shakespeare worked. Old Mr Beeston, who died in the same year as Lacy, 1682, was the son of Christopher Beeston who had been one of the Lord Chamberlain's Men and is mentioned in the cast list of Ben Jonson's *Every Man in his Humour* produced by that company in 1598. The 'principall comedians' named were headed by Shakespeare, Burbage, Phillips, Heminge, Condell, Pope, Sly, Beeston, Kempe, and Duke. Since Beeston was not mentioned in the list of the principal actors in Shakespeare's plays given in the First Folio, his stay cannot have been long or his contribution important. With Kempe and Duke he left the Chamberlain's Men soon after 1600 for Worcester's Men. Later he became owner of the Cockpit Theatre. He could have had his grievances when he was a minor colleague of Shakespeare and the others, but he had been a member of the great and memorable 'fellowship' when Shakespeare was reaching the summit of his career as a dramatist. What he told his son must have been interesting and may have been accurate. He went on to be a considerable figure in the Jacobean theatre when Worcester's team became Queen Anne's Men in 1616. He had a large share in taking over and running the Cockpit which was mentioned by Heminge and Condell in their introduction to Shakespeare's First Folio. The high opinion of Shakespeare's performance attributed to him is useful evidence. To depreciate is easier than to praise and, since Beeston had moved elsewhere, he could have made slighting remarks about one of the men who had not made him a Sharer.

The belief that Shakespeare 'did act exceedingly well' therefore had this valuable but belated authority behind it. The references to his performance made in his own time are few. Henry Chettle, a printer who became a dramatist, described him as 'excellent in the quality he professes', but Chettle was apologising for Greene's jealous and spiteful attack on the 'upstart crow, beautified with our feathers' daring to invade the aviary of the quill-men who wrote the plays and resented intrusion on what they wished to be 'a closed shop'.

Chettle in 1592 could hardly have paid so warm a compliment if Shakespeare had only been a small-part man in his early years on the stage and had never proved his abilities in a major role before that date. It would be difficult to prove excellence without a sizeable part in which to prove it. So at least a few big assignments are indicated. John Davies of Hereford wrote in 1610 that 'Will played some Kingly parts in sport', a remark which can carry any meaning we like to give it. The 'Kingly' parts in Shakespeare's own plays are frequently large ones: if such a cryptic observation can be taken seriously it implies major responsibilities in the cast. But this light-hearted rendering of royal roles may have been confined to other men's work. The cryptic comment need not be applied to the dramatist's participation in his own plays.

The idea of Shakespeare as an inconsiderable actor was started by Nicholas Rowe in 1709. In this first biography of the man whose works he was editing Rowe drew on the memories of Thomas Betterton (1635–1710) who was said by Pepys to have acted Hamlet with a skill 'beyond imagination'. The rule of the Puritans had driven acting underground and broken the line of tradition in Shakespearian performances. But Betterton was a student of theatrical practice. His memories of what had been are not to be despised. According to Downes, who was a book-keeper and prompter in 1662, Betterton got his instruction in the part of Hamlet from D'Avenant who had seen Taylor who followed Burbage in the part.

Rowe said that Shakespeare was first engaged as an actor 'in a very mean rank'. There is nothing surprising in that. The young man, whether or not he arrived in London with a touring company on its way to the capital or came independently to town to seek work, would have to begin as one of the Hired Men who doubled and trebled small parts. The number of minor roles needed especially in the historical plays and tragedies with battle-scenes required an abundance of this apprentice labour which was very poorly paid. Rewards were generally low. A Hired Man was employed at ten shillings a week on which he must have been able to live. If he was in luck he might get twelve. There were constant rehearsals, since new plays were rapidly required, and in the performances the quick-change Hired Men had a hectic time in the tire-room as they raced from one role to another. The life which Shakespeare encountered in his 'mean rank' years was hungry, strenuous and uncertain since Plague could close the London theatres, sometimes for a year or more.

The work, when it was there, was a valuable experience for a hard-working and ambitious recruit. There was no Dramatic Academy turning out promising Prize Men who get their first assignments with a medal to their credit. The senior players took the boys into their homes for professional schooling and drilled the Hired Men during rehearsals. Promotion from the 'very mean rank' was quite swift in Shakespeare's case. If he came to London, as is generally supposed, in 1588, by 1595 he had risen to be one of the few Sharers, who were the responsible leaders of the company and could make good money in times of success. The Chamber Account recorded payments made then to Kempe, Shakespeare, and Burbage. He had authority and responsibility. Chettle's complimentary statement about Shakespeare's 'excellence' as an actor was made two years earlier and confirms the impression of a rapid and steady advance in skill and status.

Rowe added to his remarks about a humble entry that 'the top of his performance was the Ghost in his own *Hamlet*'. There was a later legend reported by a biographer and antiquary, William Oldys (1691–1761), that one of Shakespeare's younger brothers had seen him play Adam in *As You Like It*. Unfortunately there is no contemporary information about the parts which Shakespeare took in his own plays. That he did take major roles is perhaps indicated by Heminge and Condell who, in editing the First Folio, placed his name at the top of the roll of honour when they were listing 'The Names of the Principall Actors in All These Playes'. To be put above Burbage was a supreme compliment.

But without further evidence it is fair to think that the exalted position was awarded as a courtesy to the author and not as a factual recognition of frequent appearance in the 'star parts'. The preface contains no other reference to the justly praised author as a player. Ben Jonson's famous salute to the Swan of Avon says nothing about his work as an actor. The line about Shakespeare's 'buskin' treading and shaking the stage might perhaps be taken as a reference to the poet as player. The Ghost in *Hamlet* gave an opportunity for an impressive and frightening performance. But the buskins, introduced by Jonson in his parade of classical allusions, were probably those of the company for whom the dramatist provided his 'well-turned and true-filed lines'.

One is left puzzled. If he 'did act exceedingly well', as Aubrey recorded on hearsay evidence long after and Chettle had suggested more than thirty years before the appearance of the First Folio, Ben Jonson might have said as much. But Ben was a failed actor and failed actors are not always profuse in praise of those who have greatly pleased the critics and the public.

It is worth noting that the editors of the Folio, so eloquent about the merits of the playwright, say nothing in their Preface of Shakespeare as a player, unless the phrase 'happy imitator of Nature' be taken as a compliment to his acting as well as to the 'most gentle expression' of Nature through his 'mind and hand'. The answer to that could be that editing the text was their primary concern and that it was a sufficient recognition to give him primacy in the actors' roll of honour. If that was indeed intended as an estimate of his work as a player there could have been no higher praise. Matthew Arnold said that he out-topped knowledge; obviously he did not out-top Burbage, put second on the Folio list but known to have been the creator of Richard III, Hamlet, Othello, and Lear. But the occasions on which Shakespeare displayed supreme powers are unknown. The Ghost in *Hamlet* has some eloquence to discharge, but it is very far from being a star part.

On one point there can be no doubt. When he wrote on themes far removed from the England he knew and from the bustle of its theatres on both sides of the Thames, that world of make-up and make-believe was never far from his mind. The scene of his plays may be alien and the time remote but his choice of words and images reveal the Bankside man to whom the play was work and the actor his hard-labouring companion. It is always a fair sign of Shakespeare's subconscious mind when the emerging metaphors, similes, and comments upon life have nothing to do with the story and its period.

Theatrical allusions abound when the situations and the characters are of a kind to whom the traffic of the stage was unknown. Jaques, with his all too familiar set-piece on the theatricality of man's life, could have been a play-goer before he took to pondering in Arden and green-wood soliloquies. But what could Macbeth know of actors and acting? Did touring companies reach Inverness in A.D. 1040? Yet, at the climax of his desperate and doomed career in the north of Scotland his mind turns to the deprivation of the actors denied the survival of other artists whose words, painting, carving and music live on in the ears and eyes of posterity.

> *Life's but a walking shadow, a poor player*
> *That struts and frets his hour upon the stage*
> *And then is heard no more.*

They were poignant lines for Burbage if he played Macbeth. What was he but a shadow, evanescent and brittle, as he strode and fought through his strenuous hours with oblivion his ultimate reward?

Shakespeare, continually aware of the fragility of his craft, so powerful for a day and so insubstantial as an asset for remembrance, was devoted to this word Shadow with its still, sad music of impermanence. It crops up suddenly on the lips of Theseus in *A Midsummer Night's Dream* while Bottom and his troupe of 'hempen homespuns' are bumbling through their tragedy. Theseus has been behaving callously, interrupting with a crude jocosity the struggling performers. One expects him to be

anything but reflective in a compassionate way. Yet for a moment
he stops to ruminate and his remark is typical in phrase and feeling of Shakespeare's sympathetic genius.

It comes in as a reply and a rebuke to Hippolyta's grumbling
about the Pyramus and Thisbe mummery which she calls 'the
silliest stuff'. 'The best in this kind are but shadows—and the
worst are no better if imagination amend them.' The author who
can feel for the actors and not the insensitive Athenian is speaking.
The audience is asked to realise the plight of the players and such
sympathetic co-operation is not usual when a performance is
becoming a mess. That Theseus should be suddenly and improb-
ably responsive to the players' distress is in sharp contrast with
his previous taunting of the blundering amateurs. The public
must be made conscious of the pains felt by the earnest and suffering creatures striving to make real their shadowy world of
illusion and pretending.

Puck apologetically ends the play with the same thought in
mind. 'If we shadows have offended . . .' That was another
problem of the actors in Shakespeare's time. They had to be
extremely careful in the presence of the great. In this case nothing
tactless must be said during the mimed celebration of a royal
wedding in a play almost certainly written for an Elizabethan
nobleman's marriage. The players had the power to hurt as well
as to enchant. Their stage was thin ice and there could be a sad
loss of occupation if it broke.

Acting is more than imitation, but it begins with that and
should, when the dramatist provides the great opportunity, be
larger than life. It can become mimicry raised to a higher power,
a revelation of truth in a character and of the inner and deeper
meaning of a story. Out of the shadows there comes a blaze of
light, but the illumination demands much of the player. Shakespeare realised the conflict of the actor's capacity with the task set
by the playwright. A curious instance of that occurs in Cleopatra's praise of her lost Antony. With a curious swerve into the
language of the theatre and its problem of giving the urgency of
the actual and substantial to pretended, shadowy people and to

fictional events she describes her lover's quality as out-ranging imagination,

> *Nature wants stuff*
> *To vie strange forms with fancy. Yet t'imagine*
> *An Antony were nature's piece 'gainst fancy,*
> *Condemning shadows quite.*

Shakespeare's mind raced in his later work and the metaphors run into one another. Here the thought and words are involved. There is an implicit indication that any player of Antony will be put to a most exacting test. Poor shadow, he will be 'o'er-parted' and liable to condemnation for failure. And so with Cleopatra herself. She has been allotted many of the finest words ever written by her author and a superhuman splendour in her courage as well as in her sensuality. These colossal roles have sometimes proved to be beyond the reach of performance by even the most gifted 'shadows'.

The pains of the actor who has been given a part beyond his scope are several times brought to mind. The point is made gently and amusingly in *Love's Labour's Lost*. The oddly assorted mummers in Act V are seeking to present to an audience including royalty, lords, and ladies a pageant-play of the Ancient Worthies. Poor Sir Nathaniel, the mild curate, is faced with the challenge of impersonating Alexander the Great. The clown Costard says to the bewildered, tongue-tied and trembling ninny: 'A conqueror and afeared to speak. Run away for shame, Alisander. (*Sir Nathaniel retires*) There, an it will please your worships, is a foolish, mild man: an honest man, look you, and soon dashed. He is a marvellous good neighbour, sooth, and a very good bowler. But for Alisander, you see what it is, a little o'erparted.' It is a charming and kindly excuse for the victim of a ridiculous assignment. There is no reason why Costard should know the dilemma of professionals casting a play with sadly inadequate talent. He might have spoken more roughly of Nathaniel's failure, but the voice is that of Shakespeare, not of the rustic droll. The actor-playwright knew what might happen when one of his team was given a role above his capability and was 'soon dashed'.

The same discomfiture is mentioned in very different circumstances in *Coriolanus*. The Roman general, never shrinking from battle against desperate odds, is frightened of being 'o'er-parted' when faced by the need to be a public orator among the mob in the market-place. He protests (III, ii),

> *You have put me now to such a part which never*
> *I shall discharge to the life.*

Cominius, who has bidden him play the demagogue, replies,

> *Come, come we'll prompt you.*

The participants in the Volscian wars were battling in 490 B.C., centuries before Plautus and Terence taught the Roman public the pleasures of an acted comedy. Of course one does not look for exact chronology in Shakespeare's choice of metaphors and similes. What is striking and fascinating is the recurring recollection of the player's difficulties when his characters are in trouble. Sir Edmund Chambers, in his collected volume of *Shakespeare Gleanings*, has pointed out the frequency of theatrical images in *Coriolanus*. Of Caius Martius it is said (II, iii),

> *When he might act the woman in this scene*
> *He proved the best man in the field.*

The same tragic hero says to his wife and mother (V, iii),

> *Like a dull actor now,*
> *I have forgot my part and I am out*
> *Even to a full disgrace.*

The humiliation of the actor who 'dries' in nervousness had been alluded to much earlier in the poet's life. In Sonnet 23 occurs the simile from stage-life,

> *As an imperfect actor on the stage*
> *Who with his fear is put beside his part . . .*

34

As a playwright Shakespeare had heard his lines mauled and even murdered by the frightened wretch, o'er-parted, soon dashed and ineffectively prompted. His fellows on the stage would have told him to thribble through as best he could. (Thribble was a word used by another and minor dramatist, Richard Brome, for improvising lines.) As a player he may himself have halted in a flurry and known 'the full disgrace'. The hasty productions inevitable in his time cannot always have provided word-perfect rendering of dialogue and the long and sometimes tangled speeches. Shakespeare himself, especially in his later style when his metaphors out-raced his pen in a turbid flood, set the players some teasers.

Throughout the plays the characters are apt to see themselves as theatrical performers on the stage of history. Hamlet not only talks stage 'shop'; his mind is full of performance visualised. When recounting the way in which, 'netted round with villainies' at sea, he has escaped from the plot against his life he says,

> *Ere I could make a prologue to my brain*
> *They had begun the play.*

Later at the summit of the tragedy he sees the courtiers, who have watched the duel and its bloody termination, as play-goers,

> *You who look pale and tremble at the chance*
> *That are but mutes and audience to the act.*

Sympathetic to the man of faulty memory who stumbled amid his lines and was publicly abashed, Shakespeare also felt compassion for the minor player made to feel small in the presence of a greater one. In *Richard II* the self-dramatising King continually thinks in terms of his own life as that of a performer in a theatre. He visualises 'the antic' Death as a player with 'a little scene' in which to 'monarchize, be feared, and kill with looks'. Richard also sees himself as a versatile impersonator of widely different types.

> *Thus play I in one person many people,*
> *And none contented. Sometimes I am a king;*
> *Then treasons make me wish myself a beggar;*
> *And so I am.*   (V, v)

Earlier in the same Act he had spoken for the secondary player, the Hired Man, outshone and made to seem a dullard by the illustrious superior with his star-quality and richer opportunity,

> *As in a theatre, the eyes of men*
> *After a well-graced actor leaves the stage,*
> *Are idly bent on him that enters next*
> *Thinking his prattle to be tedious.*

Such could be the pains of those who followed a Burbage when his exit had evoked a round of applause. While Shakespeare was grandly executing his task as a dramatist in this tragedy he was constantly bearing in mind that a playwright is a partner and that the life of his creation is in the hands of his colleagues who could endanger or enhance the crucial episode and powerful line. A passage we call memorable could be ill-remembered at the critical moment.

His pity for the actors at a loss, o'er-parted, or made to seem prattlers by the spell-binding diction of the First Player undoubtedly suggests that he had sometimes had his bad moments on the stage and knew intimately the possible sufferings of 'a walking shadow'.

Rowe's statement about the Ghost in *Hamlet* does not prove that Shakespeare never had a larger part if we assess a role by the number of lines. It may well indicate that he was supposed never to have done anything better in quality of performance and that his grisly, out-of-the-grave appearance and powerful diction had been long remembered. We must not assume that, while he asked for temperance in speech and gesture as a rule, he could not lay on a bit of 'ham' (and love it) when he had written a part that asked for it. In a recent 'advanced' production of *Hamlet* the Ghost was, like Wordsworth's cuckoo, a 'wandering voice'.

Shakespeare's spooks were meant to be seen as well as heard. Hamlet Senior reappears unsepulchred 'in complete steel' and neither actor nor audience would have liked to be cheated of the clanking steps at Elsinore or of the spectral Banquo's 'gory locks' which shook Macbeth at Inverness.

If Shakespeare had been acclaimed in the star-parts in his own plays surely some mention of this would have found its way into the gossip of the time or into the tributes after his death. I shall suggest later that there was one leading role in which he saw himself as the actor because he had revealed himself as the author, not only in the characteristics attributed to the man but in allusions to his own life-story as it is revealed in the Sonnets. That was Berowne in *Love's Labour's Lost*, bewitched by the eyes and tongue of a dark lady and punning on a name notorious at the Court in the last years of the sixteenth century. The play had an early and a later version and it is a fair guess that Burbage took Berowne on the second occasion if he was unavailable for the first, not yet having joined the Chamberlain's Men. There could have been Shakespeare's chance. That may be a wild surmise, but I shall give my reasons for thinking the identification with Berowne to be likely.

That Shakespeare came up from Stratford in 1611 to play Prospero in *The Tempest* has been suggested on the fanciful supposition that he would have liked to deliver the valedictory speech containing 'Our revels now are ended' and the mention of 'the great globe itself'. But if there is a pun on the name of his company's theatre why should he include a prophecy of global dissolution and the actors vanishing into thin air? That was carrying the 'shadow' image cruelly far. Why too should he want to impersonate one who in the first Act has been introduced as a garrulous, sleep-inducing bore who twice set his daughter yawning? I would rule out the Prospero idea. Shakespeare's name appeared in no cast-list after 1603. That may be an accident. It may indicate that he had had enough of memorising other men's lines. He had plenty of his own to write and some of his most exacting themes to handle.

A reasonable inference from this scanty evidence is that as an actor he kept on the fringe of his own plays while taking large parts in Ben Jonson's. The Ghost in *Hamlet* gave Shakespeare time enough to keep an eye on the boy who played Ophelia, if he needed watching. Burbage was fully competent to make the most of the Prince but he would be glad of the author at his side since that author was not a lecturing theorist but an actor himself.

Adam is a likely part, or particle, for one with much else to think about. It would set Shakespeare free to coach the lad who had the rich opportunity of speaking Rosalind's enchanting lines. Orlando, with Burbage there, could look after himself, but the wrestling victory over a plausibly muscular Charles needed good preparation. Then there are the songs. Devoted to music, he wanted them perfectly sung. For composer, at least for one of them, he had the excellent Thomas Morley who arranged the settings for 'O Mistress Mine' in *Twelfth Night* and 'It was a lover and his lass' in *As You Like It*.

Morley was for some years a neighbour of Shakespeare's in Bishopsgate and, if still there and in good enough health (in 1597 he was an invalid and wrote that he was compelled to 'keepe at home') he could have walked across with him to a rehearsal. But a charming air does not guarantee perfect results. There was always a risk with the boy's approaching puberty. Hamlet was aware of that. He noticed that the boy player in the visiting troupe at Elsinore had grown taller by some inches since last seen. Sympathetically fearing for his continued suitability in women's parts, he prayed that his voice be not cracked. That this mishap had actually occurred during the rehearsals of *Cymbeline* is shown by an insertion of lines in Act IV, Scene 2. We have the revised text.

Arviragus and Guiderius were expected to sing the exquisite lament over Imogen wrongly supposed to be dead, 'Fear no more the heat o' the sun'. If music appropriate to its beauty had been composed the poignancy would have been intensified. But the boys' lines had to be rewritten. Says the former,

Now our voices
Have got the mannish crack

and the latter adds,

> *I cannot sing. I'll weep and word it with thee.*
> *For notes of sorrow out of tune are worse*
> *Than priests and fanes who lie.*

Why, one wonders, these anti-clerical suspicions? *Cymbeline* is a late play and Shakespeare may have been at Stratford and so did not come to London for the rehearsals. Somebody else, who seems not to have liked parsons, may have written in hurriedly the apologetic lines. Doubtless there was some cursing of the accident which had put the two trebles out of action without warning and with no replacements immediately available.

With Shakespeare as Adam he was there to cope with such misfortunes which are familiar when the parts of growing boys are introduced in modern plays. The Elizabethan Children's Companies must have had plenty of that experience. Unburdened by a large part he could deal with the problems of production, including the indication of a forest with a few token trees. The Elizabethans were not complete nudists in their stage economy. Then there was the introduction of Hymen in what might now be called a 'mini-masque'. For this finale he showed the minimum of enthusiasm if we can judge by the shamelessly commonplace lines which he scribbled in or allowed another to inject. Her verses were stilted, almost contemptuous, trash.

> *Peace ho! I bar confusion*
> *For I must make conclusion.*

If his fellow-Sharers insisted on Hymen intervening richly robed to provide a fragment of spectacle and satisfy a public craving for an eyeful as well as an earful he consented wearily. As Adam he was not a player exhausted by rehearsal of his own little scenes but there was no chance to relax for one who was an author, Sharer, 'guider' and actor all at once. With his cares so many his

parts written by himself had to be small. He could and did play
larger roles for other men. So he had begun and so, until he was
busy with *Othello*, he continued. After that his name no longer
appears in the cast-lists, but that does not prove a complete break
with the acting in which according to some reports he did
'exceeding well'.

CHAPTER III

Telling the Public

❦

CREATING AND contriving publicity has become a major industry. Persuading the purchaser is essential to competitive commerce; great ingenuity and enormous sums are spent on sales promotion. The money available for advertising theatrical productions is tiny compared with the vast allocations to the marketing of household necessities and the various comforts of sweetmeats, alcohol and tobacco. But the theatre receives without payment news and reviews in the Press. The value of the latter varies according to the verdicts of the critics; there is an occasional outburst of rage from an author or director of a play after a series of bad notices. But managers rarely decide to keep the Press away by sending no more of the complimentary tickets which may evoke the reverse of complimentary comments. They would rather be underrated than overlooked. Anything, they decide, is better than silence.

In any case, while ordinary commerce has to pay heavily for space in the newspapers or commercial television, the theatre has the advantage of continual free publicity in features about its coming productions and familiar or emerging personalities.

Sound radio and television confront the ears and eyes of millions with plays in text or plays in picture. Televised extracts of plays now running are injected into millions of homes, usually with rewarding results. Moreover there are constant programmes on the problems of the playwright and the player working in the live theatres. The actor and actress are in the forefront of the frequent dilemma-discussions. How did the ripe Mr A. study for his next classical role, how did the raw Miss B. become 'a star in a night'? They have ample chance to inform the world of their juvenile yearnings; the man recounts his hard grind in repertory, the girl shows her charms and tells of her lucky break.

In the incessant outpourings of the Mass Media the drama of the most serious kind and not only Show Business has a privileged position. Critical snarls are maddening to their victims but that risk has to be set against the advantages of continual publicity which is bound to be favourable if those discussed and brought to the screen use their opportunities adroitly. The best do not push for that self-promotion, but their managements have Press Agents who must earn their living by keeping their films, plays, and people in the news.

Sometimes in the strife of competition a man's best friend may be his foolish enemy. The Elizabethan players encountered the frenzied vituperation of the Puritans. If it be true that there is no such thing as a bad advertisement they had that in plenty. Those who wished to present them as the wickedest of men naturally made them seem exciting by the screams of horror in the pulpit and by the extravagance of the pamphleteers.

Everything was done to create the image of freakish deformities and bestial habits with no understanding that freaks and animals are the successful showman's stock-in-trade. The actors were presented as the creatures of a weird menagerie. Among the enemies of human life to which they were likened were crocodiles, wolves, and vipers. Pestilential insect life was introduced into the vocabulary of vituperation. They were drones, wasps, caterpillars, mites and maggots.

The early leader of the hysterical attack had been Stephen Gosson whose *Schoole of Abuse, containing a pleasaunt invective against Poets, Pipers, Players, Jesters and such like Caterpillars of a Commonwealth* was published in 1579. At least he wrote of what he knew since he had been a player himself, sinning and repenting at leisure. When he became a clergyman he let fly at his old associates as 'dancing Chaplines of Bacchus'. But at least he admitted the possibility of some quality in a serious play. Philip Stubbs, whose book, *The Anatomy of Abuses*, included 'A summary of the Notable Vices', raged particularly at the profanation of Sunday

by the luring of people from the word of God to 'theatres and
unclean assemblies' whose plays 'were sucked out of the devil's
teats'. Of the play-house he said that it was the Palace of Venus
and a Synagogue of Satan where were spectacles of whoredom to
inflame the passions and weaken the will.

Stubbs added to the liberties of random love-making the in-
iquities of the Cities of the Plain. The play-goers, he said, became
'Sodomites or worse'. By this reckless misrepresentation of what
was to be seen and heard in a theatre the men of righteousness
supplied every kind of temptation to lusty youth in search of
forbidden pleasures, and that pursuit is a normal diversion of the
adventurous juvenile. The apprentice class was then notorious for
its holiday turbulence. Even staid seniors must have had their
fancy quickened by the lesson to be learned from the spawn of
Satan in a play-house. Here they would learn

'how to be false, and deceive your husbands, or husbands their
wives, how to play the harlots, to obtain anyone's love, how to
ravish, how to beguile, how to betray, to flatter, lie, swear,
foreswear, how to allure to whoredom, how to murther, how to
poison, how to disobey and to rebel against Princes, to consume
treasures prodigally, to move to lusts, to ransack and spoil cities
and towns, to be idle and blaspheme, to sing filthy songs of love,
to speak filthy.'

The Elizabethan actors raised a flag on the play-house roof,
sounded a drum and blew a trumpet to announce that a performance was about to begin. On tour they paraded through the
country towns as circuses long continued to do. In London they
were talked about and no doubt stimulated that conversation to
arouse curiosity. They could not employ Press Agents because
there was no Press. They could not blow their own trumpets in
the way of modern publicity. But, if the view be taken that there
is no such thing as harmful publicity, they profited by the
intemperate scolding of their enemies who denounced them in
the pulpit and railed at their wicked profession in books and

pamphlets. When Sir James Barrie was the principal guest at the dramatic critics' annual dinner he saw himself as a playwright in a den of hospitable wolves. Surveying his hosts he charmingly began to address them with the word 'Scum'. Shakespeare and his kind were not only scum to the Puritans: they were the targets of tirades which used the full resources of the English language then raised to its highest power.

Did the players realise with delight and gratitude that this was enhancing their attraction? The furious clerics used language so extreme as to arouse public interest in the theatre, which they described as Satan's workshop. If the actors were such monsters of depravity surely any lively fellow with a taste for exciting entertainment would be curious to discover what enormities of sin were on view and what alluring vices could be enjoyably acquired. If the fulminating preachers did not realise that they were inviting an audience which they sought to discourage they must have been blind indeed to the workings of crowd-psychology. The stream of abuse had begun in the fifteen-seventies and eighties and was still in flux at the end of Shakespeare's career. In 1615 a cleric who signed himself 'I.G.' lashed the players with his arraignment of idlers whose day's work was two hours of 'vain babbling' and even demanded the public whipping of all such strollers who, though charged with loafing, were so busy with debauchery.

Gosson had explained that the public would enjoy 'wonderful laughter and shout together with one voice' when they 'saw some notable cozenage practised or some sly conveyance of bawdry brought out of Italy'. (It was long an English habit to put the blame for indecency on the foreigners.) Also in the audience, as he described it, there was 'such heaving and shoving, such itching and shouldering to sit by women . . ., such tickling, such toying, such winking, such smiling, such manning them home when the sports were ended'. Without knowing it he was advertising the devices of the Devil to all the prurience of youth on the spree with the assurance of a giggle or a guffaw at the gags and intrigues of those whom Nashe, a theatre man, called 'the squirting bawdy comedians'. It is true that Shakespeare had not emerged when the Puritan preachers were in their full and foolish cry. But the sermons did not cease to emphasise this kind of attraction for the crude and callow frequenters of the play-house.

This was the way to fill at least the cheaper parts of the theatre, and it would certainly not deter the sophisticated graduates who left the Universities at sixteen or seventeen to become 'termers' at the Inns of Court where seasonal revels were a regular and riotous feature of their 'further education'. They were an important element in the theatre public; they had money in hand as well as a taste for the poetry and passions of the drama. The players must have been careful to keep this source of support informed about their new and forthcoming productions.

Northbrooke, indicting Satan's tricks 'to bring men and women into his snare of concupiscence and filthie lustes of wicked whoredome', mentioned the advance publicity gained by the players setting 'bills upon postes certain dayes before'. In this they were following the practice of the managers of the Bear Garden whose bills advertised such spectacles as 'The wearying a bull dead at the stake and pleasant sport with the horse and ape and whipping of the blind bear'. Such was the rival attraction for a play of Shakespeare's at the Globe Theatre next door to it.

A leaflet is a perishable article and its survival even for a week or two after the event is unlikely. But one has been preserved, that of a pageant-play called *England's Joy* due to be played at the Swan on November 6, 1602. Apparently and, in view of the contents, understandably, there was some chaos in its preparation and it may never have been acted at all. But the bill still exists in the keeping of the Society of Antiquaries. It is a curious document indicating good taste in the printer who gave it elaborately decorated margins. The type is small and the information ample in one regard since it details the action and spectacle of nine episodes, including the battle of the Spanish Armada, the dissipation of the Irish rebels, and a great 'triumph with fighting of twelve gentlemen at barriers'.

For culmination there was to be a vision of the Queen 'taken up into Heaven, when presently appears a Throne of blessed Soules and beneath, under the Stage set forth with strange fireworkes, divers blacke and damned Soules wonderfully described in their severall torments'. A Drury Lane melodrama of seventy years ago could scarcely have coped with such a variety of panoramas. It is not surprising that with the slender equipment and resources of an Elizabethan theatre it became 'a non-event'. That it was ever considered possible gives us a useful picture of what Elizabethan showmanship would do, if it could.

The matter of *England's Joy* is sensational, but the playbill, while it records the pageantry so hopefully planned, makes no kind of popular appeal. There is no mention of the author, the company, or of any star-player. There is no resort to bold, eye-catching type and supposedly exciting adjectives. If ever there was a theatrical production which deserved and could have been saved by a blaze of publicity it was this monstrous essay in the spectacular. Yet in its billing it was offered to the public with more of a whimper than a bang. If this was a normal example of bill-posting the craft of advertising and sales promotion was still unborn.

It is strange that in the announcement of competitive productions by rival companies there was no competition allowed. The printing of playbills was a monopoly of James Roberts, a member of the Stationers' Company who had married in 1564 the widow of John Charlewood and so acquired his exclusive right to this section of the industry. The Public Relations Officers of today, clever specialists in types and layout, would have much to say about a system which tied their inventive hands in this frustrating manner.

Among the Elizabethan printers piracy of play-texts was frequent. There was no regard for the rights of the dramatist. For lack of evidence we cannot know whether there was any invasion of the privileged position enjoyed by Roberts with the sanction of the Stationers' Company. It would have been natural for the players to complain that Roberts was failing to promote their undertakings sufficiently and to look for a printer better

46

able to hit the public in the eye. Were the Shakespearian 'open-
ings' heralded by so bleak a bill with the plot of *Hamlet* or *Macbeth*
recounted in unimpressive detail and not a word about the
playwright and the players or any novel features to be expected?
Roberts's bill shows the modesty of good taste, but the theatre
cannot thrive on reticence.

It is a curious fact that the foundation of English journalism
has a link with Shakespeare through the practical activities of a
printer called Nathaniel Butter. He worked with a press and shop
at the sign of the Pied Bull in St Paul's Churchyard. Before his
time there had been some distribution of handwritten sheets
recording the news, if 'hard' news was obtainable, or gossip if it
was not. Whether they included the doings of the players is
unknown. Butter was alert as well as unscrupulous. He realised
that a leading dramatist's name was an asset on the cover of a
Quarto and proceeded to exploit it by issuing a play called *The
London Prodigal* in 1602, ascribing it to Shakespeare, and announcing that it was 'plaide by the Kings Majesties Servants'.
The latter fact was probably true since it could be easily checked.
The claim for the authorship of this comedy about a rake reformed
by his wife has generally been taken to be false since the style
betrays it. Heminge and Condell, who had intimate knowledge
of what Shakespeare did and did not write, rejected it. The text
has survived and was rashly included by Chetwynd in the Third
Folio of 1664.

Three years later Butter published the first Quarto of *King
Lear* 'as it was played before the Kings Majestie upon St Stephan's
Night in Christmas Hollidays. By his Majestie's servants playing
usually at the Gloabe on the Bancke-side.' The spelling practised
by Butter had the copious varieties of the time. There has been
much argument over the source of the text which is confused but
not much truncated since the Folio text is only longer by a
hundred lines. Butter may have got it from a short-hand writer.
(The word stenography appeared in the English language in
1602.) Managements tried to prevent theft of their valued texts
and a man in the audience who scribbled busily in short-hand on

47

his 'tables' must have been cunning if he could avoid detection and forcible ejection. However that may be, Butter got his script and issued it.

In 1622 he launched the first English printed periodical, *The Weekly Newes*, and thus was a principal founder of the industry of Fleet Street. The Italians, especially the Venetians, had been ahead of the English. They had their Coranti and Gazetti, mentioned by Ben Jonson in his comedy of 1625, *The Staple of News*. The word 'gazette' is one of journalism's imports.

This was the first of Jonson's last four pieces which have met with small praise and added more to his anger than to his renown or his income. To a student of war *The Staple of News* is fascinating because it includes some remarkable foresight about the naval and military methods of the future. Amphibian forces invading by sea do not have landing-craft but the men and horses are equipped with large cork shoes. One report from a foreign correspondent tells of a burning glass, found in Galileo's study, 'to fire any fleet that's out at sea'. Another prophetic story said that the Hollanders have made 'an automa which runs under water'. It is like 'an invisible eel', able 'to swim the haven at Dunkirk and sink all shipping there'. This prototype of submarines has 'a nimble tail' with which she bores into the sides of ships, 'a most brave device, to murder their flat bottoms'.

Home news was covered in the play by four 'emissaries'. They are described as 'Men employed outward that are sent abroad to fetch in the commodity'. Emissaries! 'A fine new word' says one of these reporters, and it is added that 'the taverns and eating-houses will help them much'. In the editorial chair sits the Examiner who sifts the copy. The areas allotted to the emissaries are described as 'four cardinal quarters', the Court, St Paul's, Exchange, and Westminster Hall, signifying, as we should say, royalty, general business, the City, and politics.

Since Jonson lived amid the traffic in books and plays it is surprising that this source of news was not deemed 'cardinal' by his imagined editor. St Paul's, where 'Master Ambler, a fine-paced gentleman', was 'to walk the middle aisle', was a general trading-place in addition to being a Cathedral. Its site was at the heart of the printing and publishing trade, so it is likely that a man with this assignment brought in some news of the arts and artists while Master Buzz of the Exchange was recording the schemes and achievements of the financial speculators. There was comment of a sarcastic kind included in their reports. The emissaries were to be 'jeerers'. If Butter was the model no doubt he could put his quill to stabbing uses. The jobs of the Jonsonian emissaries were heavily sought for since the proprietor sold them at fifty pounds each with no salaries mentioned. They would have to live on their pickings—which hardly suggests that, at least in Ben's opinion, journalism was born incorruptible.

The picture is that given by a tough satirist but Satire must begin with the facts at which it jeers in malicious fancy. The Master Ambler of Butter's periodical could help or harm a book or a play. But Jonson is not informative about that. He introduces four characters called Gossip in the prologues and epilogues of his acts. They are named Mirth, Tattle, Expectation, and Censure. In them we meet what mattered most and what only mattered to the writers and actors before Butter was a pioneer of printed journalism. That was word of mouth.

The population of London at the end of the sixteenth century is generally believed to have been about two hundred thousand of whom most adults could read and all could listen. They were thickly clustered along the Thames, living beside or over their work, close to their shops and markets, near also to Whitehall, the seats of power and the noblemen's mansions on the north river-bank between the Temple and Charing Cross. Such a community, with none of the external supply of news with which we are flooded, was a forcing ground of report garbled with rumour. With Ambler in the thronged aisles and adjacent printing-houses of St Paul's, Buzz 'on 'Change', with Everyman and his wife in the streets and shops, Elizabethan London was a gossip's paradise as Shakespeare well knew. 'Enter Rumour, painted full of tongues.' In the Induction to the Second Part of *Henry IV* he eloquently described the winds of false report in which 'continual slanders ride'. He mentioned particularly their effect on

> *The blunt monster with uncounted heads*
> *The still-discordant, wavering multitude.*

But the rich, except those round the throne to which came the carefully protected and probably reliable despatches of ambassadors, were not much better equipped to separate fact from fiction. They, like the multitude, had to accept scrappy and slowly collected news and judge its value as best they could. In the clatter of town life they inevitably depended on the tattlers.

If the actors had had money to spare on advertisement they would providently have employed their own emissaries to scatter information about forthcoming productions and scatter favourable report about their plays then to be seen. Their natural ground for sowing this seed was in the Inns of Court, the ale-houses, and the eating-places. The bills were posted up here and there but, on the evidence of the only one we have, they were colourless. That the players could spread a good valuation of themselves is shown by the puff which the touring team had managed to convey to Polonius. How else could he know that they were 'the best actors in the world for tragedy, comedy, history' and all mixtures thereof? Rosencrantz and Guildenstern, typical tattlers of the time, had been told of their coming. Somebody had been succeeding with 'advance publicity'.

There was an extremely wide range of eyes and ears to be reached and of tongues to be set talking. The kind of play-goer most desired was described by John Marston:

> *Now I have him that ne'er of ought did speak*
> *But when of plays and players he would treat.*

There was the perfect member of an audience, the garrulous devotee. The author of the introduction to the Second Quarto of *Troilus and Cressida*, 'A never writer to an ever reader', mentioned the 'dull and heavy-witted worldlings' who, once incapable of the wit of a comedy, parted from one of Shakespeare's 'better witted then when they came'. They had come to this quickening experience 'by report'. Some tongues had done good work.

The 'rough monster' of Rumour's wavering multitude who had spent his penny to be a groundling was quite as likely to be appreciative in his talk of a new play as was the cultivated patron in the galleries. Dekker's jeering Gull paid sixpence for a seat on the stage where he smoked, ate, was talkative, sardonic, and boisterous. But the Inns of Court men had manners and the gossip of the gentry and that of those who had taste as well as money was valuable. Ben Jonson, in his commendatory verses for Fletcher's *Faithful Shepherdess*, listed some members of

> *The many-headed Bench that sits*
> *Upon the life and death of Plays and Wits.*

He included Gamesters, Captains, Knights, and 'brave sparks' along with their servants and 'the shop's foreman'. Jonson also spoke of his own play *The Silent Woman* as fit for ladies, lords, Knights, and squires and included 'the waiting-wench'. The women's vote was important.

So was that of the foreign visitors for whom a visit to the play was an essential part of sampling London life. They were especially impressed by the liberty of the ladies to visit the play-houses and the taverns where the plays were discussed and of this they told their fellow-countrymen. From the Venetian Embassy attached to the Court of St James, Busino reported that 'These theatres are frequented by handsome ladies who seat themselves among men without the slightest hesitation'.

Shakespeare knew that to get the women talking was a dramatist's need. Two of his epilogues make a special appeal to them to spread the good news of an enjoyable outing. Rosalind, at the close of *As You Like It*, emphasises the feminine dominance in the reception of a play and 'conjures' women to be kind to it. There is a similar appeal at the end of *Henry VIII*. Will the women kindly 'smile and say 't will do'? If they are so obliging 'all the best men are ours'. 'Say' is the operative word. They must recount their approval and so put in action that rewarding Jonsonian character, Expectation. Prospero, in his final words, spoken direct to the audience, says that the players' purpose had been 'to please', a point to be noted by those who take this romantic comedy of girl-meets-boy to be profoundly doctrinal. He has previously asked for at least a favouring whisper:

> *Gentle breath of yours my sails*
> *Must fill or else my project fails.*

Project meant an investment to the new brand of Jacobean capitalists. Prospero is speaking for the King's Men who had put up the money for what, with its magical effects and its masque, must have been a costly bit of projecting. His request is for subsequent talk as well as for present hand-claps.

Jeerers were not wanted, but tattlers were. The garrulity of Marston's play-house addict and unquenchable chatter-box was one of the stimulants without which the finest poetry would be wasted on the cold air of empty houses. There could be, according to many of the pamphleteers, a deplorable lack of silence in the theatre when the sixpenny sparks were being facetious and 'mewing' at the actors. They were a nuisance but at least they had paid sixpence for their seats. Far more damaging would have been silence outside the theatre. During Shakespeare's life in the theatre, without newspapers and gossip columns, with the playbills so austere, and in a town that was a string of gossiping villages, the spoken word was sovereign.

CHAPTER IV

To the Barber's

POLONIUS, AFTER listening to the turgid eloquence of the First Player, remarks as sensibly as tersely, 'This is too long.' To that Hamlet tersely and somewhat rudely replies, 'It shall to the barber's with your beard.' He has been talking as a practical critic of plays and players and as one who knows the theatrical fashions and favourites of the London stage. Since he has taken the cutting of a speech for granted and since the Prince in Elsinore is here the mouthpiece of the author in London it is obvious that Shakespeare regarded some trimming and curtailing as normal. Hamlet has no word of sympathy for the actor thus slighted and deprived of his big opportunity without being consulted.

That was all in the day's work. All had to face the risk, even the probability, of being cut down to size. Here, for example, is a dramatist's explanation of a text given in full after the barbers had been snipping. When John Webster's *The Duchess of Malfi* appeared in a Quarto edition ten years after its production it was announced as the 'perfect and exact Coppy with diverse things printed that the length of the Play would not beare in the Present-ment'. Webster may have gnashed his teeth as his 'diverse things', jewels to him, were treated as time-consuming superfluities. But he did not venture to complain. He had got his 'presentment' and his fee; he had been privileged with a production including the best players of the time as the cast-list showed. Many lines may have been missing, but Burbage was there. Without the actors' approval of the whole and removal of some the Duchess might never have spoken her lines of unforgettable courage and defiance and those lines, without public performance, would never have been printed. By an apt coincidence Bosola says in the following Act:

> *We are merely the stars' tennis-balls, struck and bandied*
> *Which way please them.*

Star was not then a term in theatrical talk, but the stars, as we understand them, were ready to make tennis-balls of the playwrights. Webster had been knocked about the court, perhaps even when he thought he had served an 'ace', and Shakespeare shared that experience of the play-game.

He knew that he might have the scissors applied to his work and there can be little doubt that some of his plays, and *Hamlet* not least, had to be given the barber's treatment. When he was not so gripped by a subject that his thoughts and felicity of language were in flood there may have been only a snip or two. But at times when his mind raced he forgot the play-house necessities and the possible impatience of the audience. Since the texts of both the Second Quarto and the Folio of *Hamlet* considerably outrun the usual playing-time of the Elizabethan theatre it is likely that the removal of hair deemed superfluous by his colleagues was more than a gentle combing out.

Hamlet is the longest of his plays. Its fullest text is estimated at over 3,750 lines. (Mixture of prose and verse makes precise calculation difficult.) The First Quarto, issued in 1603, need not be considered here since it was a garbled and mutilated version probably sold, because of its immediate success, by an ill-paid minor actor for a small but useful payment to the piratical printers Ling and Trundell. They announced that it had been 'diverse times acted' by the Chamberlain's and King's Men in London, Cambridge, and Oxford. If it was played as printed in this Quarto it was a grotesque shadow of its real self. The cutter had been as murderous as melodrama's Sweeney Todd, 'the Demon Barber of Fleet Street'.

The Second Quarto was issued in the following year to put the matter right. It was printed by Roberts, the playbill monopolist, and Ling who had apparently been useful and forgiven for his offence. It was described as 'Newly imprinted and enlarged to almost as much againe as it was, according to the true and perfect Coppie'. This suggests that the manuscript had been supplied by Shakespeare. For the First Folio Heminge and Condell evidently used a play-house copy, slightly cut, since their text was two hundred lines shorter. We cannot be certain that there were no other cuts in the day-to-day productions at the Globe. The slightly truncated Folio text of more than 3,500 lines is far above Shakespeare's normal length and could not be given in anything like the normal playing-time.

That raises the much-discussed question of the usual duration of a performance in the Elizabethan and Jacobean theatres. The evidence is confused. In 1594 there had been a dispute among the authorities about the time taken up by the players who were regarded as a nuisance by the Lord Mayor. The Lord Chamberlain, Hunsdon, promised that his men would begin at two and finish between four and five. That suggests two-and-a-half hours as a usual length. In 1597 came the First Quarto of *Romeo and Juliet*, a cut version which was some eight hundred lines shorter than the Second Quarto of 1599. The latter was described as 'newly corrected, augmented and amended'. In the First Quarto's prologue was the well-known mention of 'the two hours' traffic of our play'. There had been severe cutting to meet that schedule. But evidently Shakespeare had later on put up a successful fight against the tyranny of the clock. The two hour limit might suit some. It did not suit him.

The information afforded by other playwrights varies. Beaumont and Fletcher mention two hours for one of their plays and that was the usual timing of a production by the Children's Companies. Dekker, concerning a comedy of his which contained 2,700 lines, promised his public 'three hours of mirth'. Ben Jonson in the Induction to the vast sprawl of *Bartholomew Fair* appealed to the audience to be ready for a long sitting. He asked its members to 'covenant and agree to remain in the places their money or their friends have put them with patience, for the space of two hours and a half and somewhat more'. In this request for tolerance in a long session there is a hint that play-goers did sometimes groan, like Polonius, 'This is too long', and suit their action to their grievance by leaving before the end.

Bartholomew Fair is six hundred lines longer than *Hamlet*. Jonson in flood, not a speedy but a steady torrent, was even more prolific than Shakespeare at full stretch. The researches of an indefatigable statistician, Alfred Hart, were cited by Sir Edmund Chambers in a fascinating chapter of his *Shakespeare Gleanings*. Hart had worked it out that in the great period of theatrical fertility, 1594–1616, Jonson wrote eleven plays averaging just under 3,600 lines. During that time Shakespeare's output was thirty-two plays averaging a little less than 2,800 lines. By examining with indomitable endurance one hundred and thirty-six plays by thirty-one other dramatists Hart found their norm to be under 2,500 lines. Jonson was the plodding Marathon man. Shakespeare, by comparison with the rest of them, was in the long-distance class, while writing more rapidly.

We can make some estimate of the amount of cutting needed if we accept two-and-a-half hours as the usual playing-time. To do so we must remember the chancy nature of theatrical performance. By reading the texts at his own pace and allowing ten minutes for pauses Hart decided that a play of 2,400 lines could be performed in two hours. One cannot challenge the arithmetic but a play-house is not a counting-house. In the case of a comedy which is going well with actors who are 'milking' their laughs, ten minutes can easily be added to the timing previously assessed at rehearsals. The amount of 'business' inserted as the performances mature is another important factor. Shakespeare's clowns knew all about that. The Elizabethan tragedies and history plays include numerous and presumably popular duels, processions, marching and counter-marching in skirmishing and battles. There was relish of a lusty scrimmage well continued. The 'flourish and alarum' routine took time as well as energy. There was an appetite for spectacle as well as rhetoric. As the fashion for masques increased these were included in a play already long, e.g. *Cymbeline*. There is the lavish pageantry described in detail in the stage-directions of *Henry VIII*. There is little value in calculations based on reading the lines in seclusion.

The clowns could scamper and, if a tumble won a laugh, repeat it with a gag added. Since there is so much reference to the 'strutting' of Elizabethan players the tragedians cannot have galloped through their scenes. They had to speak clearly (few if any in the audience knew the play in advance) and that meant no gabbling. Any serious dramatist wants his words distinctly and clearly spoken. The modern actor's fashion for seeming to be natural by throwing a line away would not have been tolerated by Shakespeare even though he were critical of booming. He had something to say and, when Hamlet asked for smoothness, he did not mean whispering.

Bernard Shaw insisted on deliberate performance with clarity in mind. No Shavian word was to be missed if he had a say in the direction. If that took time, no matter. His audience had to stick it out and he was confident that his public was happy in being patient. At the close of the Preface to *Saint Joan* he met critical complaints about excessive length. 'I have', he wrote, 'gone to the well-established classical limit of three and a half hours continual playing, barring the one interval imposed by considerations which have nothing to do with art.' He believed that quantity as well as quality was demanded or at least agreeably accepted by 'the patrons on whom I depend for my bread' and he argued that his audiences were quite different from those who could bear no more than the two-and-a-quarter hours usual in fashionable comedies. So nothing was to be rushed. Only triviality needs to be hustled along to conceal its emptiness.

Incidentally this resulted in a very slow, protracted and damaging first night for *Heartbreak House* when it opened in London, about which Arnold Bennett angrily complained. Since Shaw's death the Public Trustee who, with the advice of the Society of Authors, handles his rights, has agreed that carefully selected cuts can be made, as specified, in some of the later, longer and disquisitory plays. Shaw could have seen the reason for this. He wanted as many people as possible to receive his various messages for mankind. Art for him was essentially didactic. Therefore if repertory companies, civic theatres, and others were avoiding revivals of his longer work because of its length they might be encouraged to produce them in slightly shorter form and so spread the doctrine.

Shakespeare would have seen the point of meeting the public with a pair of scissors handy. He was an actor and a Sharer, working closely with colleagues and with them keeping an eye on the theatre's takings. He was curiously careless about his scripts. If their length was challenged as burdensome by the company and deterrent to the public I cannot see him defying them and shouting 'Not a word to be cut'. If there were cuts to be made he was there to be his own barber.

One play which comes at once to mind in this connection is *King Lear*. Did King James and his gaiety-loving Queen indeed sit through every word of it when it was their surprising choice for the Christmas revels at Court? Concerning this play Sir Edmund Chambers, in the essay already mentioned, recounted a most interesting correspondence with Granville-Barker and Lewis (later Sir Lewis) Casson who had together directed a production at the Old Vic in 1940. They had estimated that their acting text of 3,071 lines would take just two-and-a-half hours at an average rate of twenty lines a minute. In fact the performance lasted forty minutes longer with an average rate of sixteen lines to the minute.

Casson thought that the Elizabethan actors spoke more 'trippingly on the tongue', as Hamlet advised his visiting players. But that their general pace was faster than that of today can be questioned, especially as dragging the feet and gesturing with the arms (sawing the air, as Hamlet put it) were common faults. That Shakespeare's own company complied with Hamlet's counsel cannot be certain. In any case the full text of that play is an unmanageable monster except for experimental occasions. When it was given at the Old Vic in 1937, without act-intervals, it took four hours and twenty-two minutes. The slight cuts of two hundred lines in the Folio version would make little difference to that gigantic session.

There is the problem of intervals. Actors with enormous parts need them just as much as audiences with thirsts, stiff limbs, and other weaknesses. The player with a huge assignment can be given time to recover breath by a dramatist who knows his business. The gruelling role of Macbeth gets its respite in Act IV. Malcolm's somewhat verbose intervention was not one of the portions cut in an unusually short tragedy which, it is usually agreed, the Folio editors printed from a cut version. He had to be at least moderately long-winded while Macbeth was getting his wind back. The fourth Act also provides a substantial relief for Hamlet who has had very little chance to rest his voice and energy before that and has the strenuous climax to come. After the 'How all occasions' soliloquy he is rescued by the madness and death of Ophelia and by the otherwise too wordy colloquy between the King and Laertes in Act IV, Scene 7.

Shaw realised that he was asking too much of his Joan if he did not give her some time to rest in her dressing-room in the middle of her enormous and exacting part. Hence Scene 5 set in Warwick's tent, never a favourite with the average play-goer who is given a history-lesson on the menace of Joan's individualism to the secular and feudal establishment as well as to the supreme authority of the Church in matters of faith and conduct. It is, of course, Shaw at his best as an expositor. But it is also an act of mercy to his actress.

That kind of interval does not help those in the audience who are getting fidgety. For them, as Shaw reluctantly admitted, there must be a break. It seems to be generally thought that the Elizabethans drove straight on, but that there were intervals at Shakespeare's Globe is indicated by Thomas Platter, the Swiss traveller who made a careful and valuable record of his visit to England and of his stay in London in 1599. In September, 1599, about two in the afternoon he was ferried across the river to a theatre with a thatched roof on the South Bank where he saw a play about Julius Caesar. He did not mention the author but the date is exactly right for Shakespeare's tragedy. The perilous thatch was that which caused the Globe's fatally destructive fire during a performance of *Henry VIII* in the summer of 1612.

He recorded that *Julius Caesar* was splendidly performed by a cast of 'some fifteen' which shows the amount of doubling and trebling of roles by the Chamberlain's Men—and leaves one wondering about the crowd and battle scenes. He added that after the play four of the company, two dressed as men and two as women, danced most gracefully. The jig, of which Shakespeare was no friend, followed even Roman tragedy. Platter did not specify an interval or intervals but he noted the catering arrangements. 'During the performance food and drink are carried round the audience, so that for what one cares to pay one may also have refreshment.' Variety of payment suggests variety of victuals. Unless there were intervals that double service could not have been supplied without creating an outrageous nuisance to the actors and to those who had paid to listen to a play. There was already interruption enough from the waggish dandies with their sixpenny seats on the stage without the clatter of mugs, glasses, and plates.

It is possible that the only interval in *Julius Caesar* came before the jig while the battlefield was being cleared and the corpse-disposal squad was at work. But the procedure described by Platter makes another break seem likely. The Globe was in business and the Sharers, owning the equivalent of the modern and usually profitable theatre bars, would make the best use of their opportunity among the customers who paid 'as they cared' for their range of food and drinks. Was there only one pause at the end of the afternoon before the jiggers replaced the strutters? That would not satisfy the business manager. It was the custom of the people in the cheaper parts of the house to bring their own snacks and confectionery. The Citizen's Wife in *The Knight of the Burning Pestle* has come equipped with liquorice, sugar-candy and green-ginger. She sends her husband out for ale. The occupants of the 'lords' boxes' and their ladies might not care for that sort of humble do-it-yourself catering. One can imagine cries for sack and the answer 'Anon, sir, Anon' muttered to such orders by a flustered 'drawer', as occurred in the Boar's Head when Falstaff and his company were thirstily imperative. If there was this commotion the actors could insist on a pause and a cup for themselves in the tiring-room.

If we are to think of two refreshment intervals, one in the middle of the play and another before the jig, we realise still further the difficulties of play-timing. There is no Quarto, good or bad, to help us in the case of *Julius Caesar*, but since the Folio text is unusually short for a history or tragedy Heminge and Condell may have used a play-house copy on which the barber had already been at work.

We have two versions of another play of the same period and probably of the same year. The existence of alternative texts adds to our ideas about the cutting problem. The Globe was opened early in 1599, probably with *Henry V*. As rarely happens with Shakespeare's plays this piece can be closely instead of approximately dated. The evidence is provided by the reference in the second Prologue to the hopeful departure for Ireland of 'the General of our glorious Empress', the Earl of Essex, who is expected to bring rebellion 'broached on his sword'. Essex and his troops left London on March 27. It was meant as a happy topical allusion but it was sadly optimistic. The Earl came back humiliated to his angry Empress in September. Therefore the over-confident salute made later after his outset could not be made without derision. At the time of his return *Julius Caesar* was being given at the Globe and, if there were repeat performances of *Henry V*, these lines of the Prologue must have been tactfully removed and it is quite likely that the Prologues never were spoken. If Platter's visit to the Globe had been earlier in the year he could have seen *Henry V*, but it is doubtful whether he would have heard the full and lengthy text as it appeared twenty-four years later in the Folio.

The First Quarto of *Henry V*, printed by Thomas Creede, appeared in 1600. It is one of those classified by the Shakespearian specialists as 'Bad'. Some think it was a patchy version taken down in the theatre by a text-thief using short-hand or put together from bits remembered by one or more of the actors. Creede, as was noted in his association with Butter in claiming *The London Prodigal* as Shakespeare's, was in this line of sly business. In 1595 he had made another such attribution by issuing *The Lamentable Tragedie of Locrine* and describing it as 'newly set foorth, overseene, and corrected by W.S.'. Does 'set foorth' imply authorship as well as editing? Was W.S. Shakespeare? Who else could it have been? The play is fustian stuff and cannot have been his. One thing is certain. Roberts had entered a text of *Henry V* at Stationers' Hall in August 1600 in order to prevent printing by pirates. But Creede defied him, got ahead of him, and followed up his 'Bad Quarto' of 1600 with a replica in 1602.

Creede's text is only two-thirds of the length of that used by Heminge and Condell. Dr Dover Wilson believed the Folio text to have been 'printed from the manuscript as Shakespeare handed it to his company'. That can well be agreed but it does not prove that the company played it in the form in which it was received. It has been held by some that the drastically abbreviated First Quarto was indeed the acting version used by the Chamberlain's Men and that *Henry V* had been sent to the barber's without delay. Gone were the speeches of the Chorus, so fascinating to us for their typically Shakespearian style and the revelation of his longing for the grandiose realism which his new theatre could not provide and on which the Victorian and Edwardian actor-managers could and did spend handsomely. Gone were three whole scenes and some long speeches. It would have been reasonable for the players to decide that the full text was too long and that the first Act was too wordy. They could also decide that Will was going too far. To admit that the production would be wretchedly inadequate to the stirring military events showed the candour of an author who felt frustrated by his primitive stage, 'this unworthy scaffold'. But for the company it was an insult to the men and their methods. To call them 'flat, unraised spirits' was bad enough. To announce that the English army would consist of

> *Four or five most vile and ragged foils*
> *Right ill-disposed, in brawl ridiculous,*

was to let the public know that the showmanship was wretched and that it would be getting a poor deal for its money. It was possible, perhaps, for Chorus to speak the lines with a shrug of the shoulders and look for a laugh. But would the members of the team take it as a joke? It is not surprising if the Prologues were dropped. They are glorious stuff to our ears, but we are not in a hurry. The actors, if they had to get through the play in two or two-and-a-half hours at the most with refreshment intervals and a jig, had to get a move on.

That meant cutting the cackle and getting on to the imaginary steeds, regretting the inability to bring in actual cavalry. There is undeniably some prolixity in the play, especially at the start. The first Prologue suggests a torrent of military action, but there is a stream of eloquence before we get to the heart of the matter. The ecclesiastics have a case to put to justify the King's aggression, but they do spin it out. Canterbury delivers a lecture on the similarity of human activity to that of the honey-bees. It is beautifully written, being Shakespeare's. No other would have seen and heard the humming hive-makers as 'Singing masons building roofs of gold'. In this speech His Grace orates for twenty-five lines before he reaches the decisive 'Therefore to France, my liege'. Burbage, if he played the King and wanted to get on to his big scenes, could mutter 'Enough of this. It shall to the barber's', take Shakespeare aside, and ask him to slice away, even to the extent of the much diminished Quarto text. This, I surmise, was what the first audience was given. The author's full text was preserved. Heminge and Condell luckily had it and used it.

They claimed to preserve Shakespeare's plays 'absolute in their numbers, as he conceived them'. But for one of the greatest tragedies, *Macbeth*, they lacked Shakespeare's original manuscript and had to print the acting version. This contained only 2,084 lines, which must be compared with the 3,750 of the Second Quarto of *Hamlet*. If the full text of *Macbeth* had been up to this size, as is probable since the other great tragedies all approached that length, more than a third had been cut.

What exactly happened in this case has been much debated.

The various views and possibilities are discussed fully and wisely in the second section of Dover Wilson's edition of the play (Cambridge University Press, 1947). There obviously had been much intervention during the preparation of the first and sub-sequent productions. Dover Wilson reasonably believes that Court performances demanded shorter versions of the plays, especially if there were foreign guests with small, if any, know-ledge of English. He plausibly mentions the visit in 1606 of King Christian of Denmark, brother of King James's Queen Anne. The King's Men would have to stage a play on that occasion and brevity would be helpful. So much was sacrificed, some of it no doubt incomparable. One is left wondering what happened to the other great tragedies. Did the King and Queen hear only two thousand lines of *King Lear* and, if they ordered *Hamlet*, how much of that was omitted to suit them? If two hours, apart from inter-vals and extras, was the expected play-time *Macbeth*, as we have it, could have been managed in just over two hours and ten minutes at sixteen lines to the minute and under two hours if the rate was raised to twenty. If *Hamlet* were given similar treatment and limited to two or at the most two-and-a-half hours Shakespeare had to remove a third of what he must have known to be as important as anything he had done.

Dover Wilson believes and provides convincing arguments to show that Shakespeare was the barber for *Macbeth*. That would be the natural and courteous procedure to be used not only for that play but whenever his fluency had exceeded his regard for the minutes and even the hour. He was one of a company that must have argued hotly at times but did not disagree to the point of breaking up. Only one of the seniors left. When Kempe decided that he had been snubbed one might say that he danced rather than walked out. The others kept their feet on the ground, a self-restrained and self-governing team. Hamlet spoke of 'a fellowship of players' and there was enough fellowship to keep the principals from schism and separation for most of their busy lives. An affronted author whose work was notably successful and considered worth stealing would have been welcome elsewhere if he felt that he was being wronged by colleagues demanding excessive cuts. Shakespeare's constancy may have been tried, but it never failed.

Burbage was a leading actor and as a Sharer had his part in the troubles as well as the rewards. He was not a dictatorial actor-manager. If he collaborated in the cutting he did so on level terms with an agreeably amenable playwright. That might not have been the case if Shakespeare had been a detached writer. But he was a professional actor who could see the company's point of view. He had his eye on 'the house'. If the paying public wanted a certain length of entertainment, he would and did trim his plays in or before rehearsal to the required size. That is a reasonable deduction from the length of the Quartos and of the Folio text of *Macbeth*.

Why should a practical man, Johannes Factotum, as he was called with a sneer, early apprenticed to a theatre workshop and staying there for much of his life, be so feckless in the length and timing of his scripts? His period had its aloof men of letters, nobility and gentry with no need to earn a few pounds to keep alive, yet fond of putting their poetry into theatrical form. There was one of them, Fulke Greville, in a big house near Stratford-upon-Avon. He was a study dramatist. Shakespeare was as much on and around a stage as in his study, and that in his early and penurious years could not be much of a place, a hole-and-corner den. He knew the rules and the ropes. He had to hustle plays into rehearsal, sometimes rehearsing and performing himself. Yet he let his text run on and so had to endure the pains of laborious cutting. Very few authors enjoy practising surgery on their own work.

Journalists are trained in the discipline imposed by space and time. They must meet the hour and fit the space. Round St Paul's and later on the Bankside the playwrights had their Grub Street. The tycoon Henslowe wanted plays in plenty. He was like an editor who sends out his reporters on immediate jobs and com-missions articles for prompt delivery. Shakespeare may have been a member of his workshop for a short time. He was certainly on the fringe of it. There he would learn not to waste his ink and his time. Another hand was wanted to knock up another act for a play in preparation by other contributors. With the Chief paying a pound an act there was no temptation to serve overweight to that tough customer. But, promoted to better company, Shakespeare forgot the old grind in the new freedom. He spread himself and overwrote.

At the end, when he was a man of leisure, he was still being generous beyond the needs of the actors. Our Folio text of *The Tempest* is short. It may have been much longer before it was commanded at Court for the revels at the betrothal and wedding of the Princess Elizabeth to the 'Prince Palatine Elector' in 1612 and 1613. It had been given at Whitehall before that in November, 1611. *A Winter's Tale* was also one of the entertainments ordered for the marriage. It is a much longer play in the Folio text and hard to fit in to the two hours or a little more routine. We may reasonably surmise drastic cutting both for the royal occasion and for the production at the Globe which Simon Forman saw in May, 1611. In one volume of the Collected Works it fills thirty-three pages. *The Tempest* fills less than twenty-four. There again the cutting may have removed almost a third of Shakespeare's manuscript if the actors were still insisting on a limit of one hundred and twenty and not more than one hundred and fifty minutes of playing-time including pauses and a song-and-dance finale.

Much of Shakespeare's public and private life is open to conjecture. One thing, however, is certain. He was thrifty and provident. The milords were reckless with their money; to be in debt and to seek refuge from their creditors by marrying a young woman with large property and prospects was customary behaviour. The middle class, to whom Shakespeare and his fellow-actors belonged, were cautious in their lives, careful in their finance, bought homes in the suburbs or the country as refuges from epidemics, and invested outside the theatre as well as in it. They did not squander. Shakespeare sent his money back to Stratford for investment in land and tithes, adding steadily to his estate. In that he was shrewd and calculating. Yet as a playwright he was extremely wasteful, a profligate of words, writing far more than was needed. There was neither caution nor thrift when he took up a pen.

That would be reasonable if he were writing and collecting his work for publication in the knowledge that it would thus survive. Ben Jonson did that. In 1616 he supervised the printing in Folio of his plays so far written. Shakespeare handed his plays to his company and took no steps at all to preserve them. Half of them were available to readers in Quarto form and some of these were pirated and roughly handled. He had been careful with his long poems written in the early fifteen-nineties which continued to be public favourites. The proofs were carefully read. Whether the publisher, Field, his fellow Stratfordian in London, had bought them outright or paid royalties for years to come is unknown. The Sonnets seem to have been issued by Thorpe without his authority.

The long poems have for us the rich quality of ingenious youth in love with the patterns and vocabulary of the verse then in fashion. But there could have been no immortality in them alone. The Sonnets are unique, fascinating and bewildering, a source of endless speculation. But myriads do not flock to Stratford because the Sonneteer was born there. To the world Shakespeare has been not only *a* dramatist but *the* dramatist. His epics have pleased and his Sonnets allured. But it is the plays which have been continually and universally admired. Legally they were the property of the players for whom he created them on the understanding that his colleagues would handle and shape them as they thought fit for the satisfaction of their public. Was he so modest about his contribution to the theatre and so completely unaware of its power to astound and enchant posterity if it were printed for survival? He could not foresee that every word would be pored over and annotated by scholars of vast learning and many countries in the centuries to come. It is very hard for us to believe that he was wholly unconscious of his work's enduring value. His innocence now seems fantastic.

To understand it we have to think our way back to a society in which, while poetry was exquisitely written and highly esteemed, plays containing poetry of splendour were not in the same class as lyrics, epics, and sonnets. They were theatre-material. Some of them were financially valuable, but none of them was seen as durable. In our own time writers of all kinds, protected by their vigilant agents and their well-conducted Trade Union, the Society of Authors, are keenly watching their contracts with publishers and theatrical managers. There is hard bargaining over rights of all kinds including the valuable 'subsidiaries' produced by film and television sales as well as paper-back editions. Accordingly it is extremely difficult to visualise the world of Elizabethan authorship in which the dramatists poured out their copious work, some of it now regarded as masterpieces, for a small immediate payment and with no thought of anything to follow. If Shakespeare believed that he was getting all that he could expect as an energetic and successful servant of his fellows in the workaday theatrical industry of 'Let's Pretend' he was accepting the usage of his period and his profession. Ben Jonson took a longer view; he was a restless and perhaps unwanted actor and stayed with no fellowship. Shakespeare did not share his pride in his work or his spirit of independence. Jonson had the wisdom to foresee the immortality of Shakespeare's plays and in the First Folio he paid his generous tribute to a man who wrote for no single age and for all time. He then made a prophecy which could not have been more accurate, but he could not have made it earlier because half the plays were still in manuscript and in private hands. Heminge and Condell made the famous forecast of permanence possible by doing what Shakespeare should have done for himself, as Ben must have thought as he penned his lines with his own self-edited Folio beside him.

By the critics of the eighteenth century Shakespeare was considered as a poet and a playwright. In the nineteenth and much more assiduously in the twentieth century there came examination and appraisal of what may be called his teaching. The word 'message' has come into fashion. Countless lectures have been delivered and books written on Shakespeare as a man with a message and on the political and philosophical ideas to be found in the plays. It is surprising that Shakespeare, if he considered himself a conceptual thinker and a sage with a creed, should have done nothing to see that his opinions should survive in print. It seems a most curious negligence which hands over prized reflections and beliefs to the actors who could cut out as tedious and time-consuming a quantity of this testament. One cannot see Bernard Shaw, the most committed 'message' dramatist of our time, working on those permissive terms.

The ideas in the plays are of two kinds, political and ethical. It is obvious that Shakespeare, as a leading member of a company attached to the Court and supervised by the Lord Chamberlain, had to commend the rule of order and degree and the national security established by the Tudor dynasty and in general continued by King James. There was no venality in that. Shakespeare could be uncommonly scathing about the 'robes and furred gowns' which cloaked misdeeds. What mattered to him was peace at home. English history had taught him the need for the strong central authority which had put an end to the shambles created by the feuding barons in the Wars of the Roses. To glorify Gloriana was not to be an abject flatterer. It was only common sense for one who saw her triumphant tenure of the throne as the principal barrier against civil war and the chaos and bloodshed of the past. The political message of the plays was of the time and for the time.

Beyond and behind that there is a more general ethical counsel against the rancour which demands and exacts violent retribution. We need not pay too much attention to Portia's 'quality of mercy' speech. It was a tit-bit for the boy who played the part and it occurs in a highly artificial climax of a court-scene with a dramatic surprise. But increasingly in the later plays there is evidence that Shakespeare regarded compassion and forgiveness as the primary virtues. The commentators especially devoted to expounding the moral implications of the plays have paid special attention to *Measure for Measure* and the cryptic character of the Duke who is both ruler and analyst of a corrupt and sinful society. Some have taken his Vienna to be a symbol of the world and the Duke to be a symbol of God. That shadowing of divinity has also been discovered in Prospero who, thought testy and punitive at the start of the play, decides that

> *The rarer action*
> *Is in virtue than in vengeance.*

After penitence there would be 'not a frown further'. Reconciliation made a steadily growing appeal to the poet in his maturity and his partial retirement. This is stale news to those who read the academic treatises. But if Shakespeare had a message of clemency and pardon and wished to drive it home in a world of savage punishments there is further reason for wondering why he was so careless about the survival of the writing which contained it. The explanation must lie in his attitude to his life-work. He was a stage-struck man, seized in youth by the excitement of the actor's life and of writing for actors. The plays were written for them, with parts to suit them and with episodes dramatically effective. A playwright's philosophy, if he had one, would seep into them as he drove ahead with his service of the stage. But the ideas were incidental to the practical necessity.

There were other vehicles for statement of opinion. The first series of Bacon's Essays, subtitled *Counsels Civil and Moral*, had appeared in 1597. London was pelted with the scoldings and indictments of the pulpiteers and pamphleteers. If Shakespeare ever turned his hand to that form of moral and political counsel nothing has been heard of it. He kept to his own line of business and made his ideas inherent in the drama, hints not exhortations. For him the play's purpose was to be a play. Let others preach.

There is another possible explanation of the slackness in his attitude to work when completed. It had come and gone like a flood. When it was done it seemed remote like a piece of life gone by. When in the mood he overwrote and overspent his energy without calculation of the number of lines written and the time spent. That may be derived from the mentions of poets in the plays. They are men possessed. Duke Theseus in *A Midsummer Night's Dream* speaks of the poet's 'fine frenzy' and likens him to a lover driven frantic and the lunatic for whom there was no cure through understanding and compassion in the Elizabethan world. In *Timon of Athens* a poet with a small part is given a few lines in which to discuss his art with a painter. He is described as 'rapt' and significantly describes his way of work. His start may be sticky, but after that comes the 'free drift' in which he 'flies an eagle flight, bold and forth on'. The 'forth on' operators may be plodders. Anthony Trollope explained that he worked for three hours at a stretch before breakfast and made a rule of turning out twelve hundred words an hour. He never, he said, 'nibbled his pen'. Many prolific authors have been early morning men. H. G. Wells was one. Shakespeare may have been another when 'rapt'. I can imagine him hard at it through a whole night, never pausing to chew his quill. 'Bold and forth on.'

Ben Jonson, who confessed to being a plodder and spoke in his Folio verses of a poet's lines cast with 'sweat', wrote in his note-book of one whose inspiration was like a raging intoxication. This man knew no calm or relaxation in his work. The golden mean was dross to him. 'When he hath set himself to writing he would join night and day and press upon himself without release, not minding it till he fainted.' Then, the spasm passed, he had violent reactions, 'took to sport and looseness and could hardly be brought back to his book'. Dover Wilson, quoting this in his brief and illuminating *The Essential Shakespeare*, thought this could well be a picture of Shakespeare because it explains 'the strong combination of minutest care with culpable negligence' in the detail and narrative of the plays and the feeble finishes in which grandeur sometimes peters out in routine couplets and almost doggerel writing. If there were these bouts of frenzied application and subsequent exhaustion to the verge of swooning they explain not only the carelessness about inconsistent characters and events but the refusal to bother, as Jonson did bother, with what followed. To say that Shakespeare had got 'someting off his chest' underrates the relief. He had torn something out of his vitals. Some authors are content and even delighted when they finish a chapter, a book, or a play. They like the look of it. Others hate the sight of it. I fancy that Shakespeare, whether satisfied or disgusted, was sick of the affair on which he pressed himself without release. He had done his best for the players; he handed over his manuscript and he was too tired to worry about what became of it. The papers, which were not a legal property, had passed out of his hands, a packet of words which in the fiery hours had been far more than an order obeyed and a contract fulfilled. Let the others get on with their job. Let them, if they must, teach him a sense of proportion by sending it to the barber's. They knew their public. So in his quiet hours did he. But there had been nights without peace, tumultuous hours. Then he wrote for himself and damn the public. Now he wanted 'sports and looseness'. It would be nice to be in his bed and possibly not alone.

He cannot always have been in that fever of swift creation. There are several Shakespeares; his working process had a chameleon quality of mutability. There was the day-to-day steady, assiduous play-house man. There was sometimes, and quite often during the years of the great tragedies culminating in *Antony and Cleopatra*, the night-by-night victim of possession and fine frenzy. It is difficult to think of any rapture in the composition of *All's Well that Ends Well*, a utility product written surely when he was low in spirit and dutifully answering a cry for something to replace a failure or fill a repertory gap. In his normally complacent way he passed over his least favourite scripts and consented to do the cutting himself. That he might still do for the plays of his heart, those 'bold and forth on' children of the mental storm, tidying up when the glorious gale had gone down.

CHAPTER V

Burbage and Others

❧❧❧

HERE IS a contemporary description of a player with star-quality.
It is headed 'An Excellent Actor'.

'Whatsoeuer is commendable in the graue Orator, is most
exquisitly perfect in him; for by a full and significant action of
body, he charmes our attention: sit in a full Theater, and you will
thinke you see so many lines drawne from the circumference of
so many eares, whiles the *Actor* is the *Center*. He doth not striue
to make nature monstrous, she is often seene in the same Scaene
with him, but neither on Stilts nor Crutches; and for his voice tis
not lower then the prompter, nor lowder then the Foile and Target. By his action he fortifies morall precepts with example; for
what we see him personate, we thinke truely done before us: a
man of a deepe thought might apprehend, the Ghosts of our
ancient *Heroes* walk't againe, and take him (at seuerall times) for
many of them.

'Hee is much affected to painting, and tis a question whether
that make him an excellent Plaier, or his playing an exquisite
painter. Hee adds grace to the Poet's labours: for what in the
Poet is but ditty, in him is both ditty and musicke. He entertaines
us in the best leasure of our life, that is betweene meales, the most
unfit time, either for study or bodily exercise: the flight of Hawkes
and chase of wilde beastes, either of them are delights noble:
but some think this sport of men the worthier, despight all
calumny. All men haue beene of his occupation: and indeed, what
hee doth fainedly that doe others essentially: this day one plaies
a Monarch, the next a priuate person. Heere one Acts a Tyrant,
on the morrow an Exile: A Parasite this man to night, to morow a
Precisian, and so of diuers others. I obserue, of all men liuing, a

73

worthy Actor in one kind is the strongest motiue of affection that can be: for when he dies, wee cannot be perswaded any man can doe his parts like him.'

This tribute was one of the additions made to the sixth edition (1615) of Sir Thomas Overbury's book of *Characters*. Sir Thomas died in the Tower, probably murdered, in 1613, and his book was enlarged by other unknown hands. This contribution has been attributed to the dramatist John Webster on grounds of style. That the actor is Richard Burbage can be assumed with some confidence owing to the mention of painting. It is certain that Burbage, despite constant appearance in the theatre, did find time for that other art. On March 31st, 1613, the Earl of Rutland's steward recorded in his accounts, 'To Mr Shakespeare in gold about my Lorde's impreso forty-four shillings, to Richard Burbage for paynting and making yt, in gold forty-four shillings.' Three years later Burbage received another payment for 'my Lorde's shelde and for the embleance'.

An impreso was an imitation shield with painted decoration and motto. It was carried by a nobleman's squire at a display of tilting. In 1613 there were festivities to celebrate the tenth anniversary of the accession to the throne of King James. Shakespeare's share in this service of the Earl was not explained by the Steward. He may have helped to devise it for Burbage's paintbrush on the first occasion. He was at Stratford and within a month of his death when the second impreso was ordered.

In 1603 John Davies of Hereford wrote of Burbage's painting in lines which link him with Shakespeare as men beloved. The portrait of a woman's head, now in the Dulwich Gallery, was catalogued as 'done by Mr Burbige, ye actor'. There is no knowledge of other players thus doubly gifted unless Shakespeare was a partner in the painting of the impreso. The vivid prose-picture must surely be that of Burbage.

There was a close link between him and Webster as actor and playwright. The latter's horrific tragedy *The Duchess of Malfi* was produced by the King's Men in 1613 or 1614 and several times revived. When it was printed in 1623 it was announced as 'Presented privately at the Black-Friers and publiquely at the Globe. The Actors Names. Bosola, J. Lowin. Ferdinand, R. Burbidge. Cardinal, J. Taylor.' At the end of the list was 'The Dutchesse', R. Sharpe. It is not certain to which of the performances these names apply. Master Sharpe may have come in too late to play any of Shakespeare's heroines. He is not included in the First Folio list of 'Principal Actors' in Shakespeare's plays.

Whoever was the author of the Character of 'An Excellent Actor' and whoever the recipient of the eulogy (Burbage, as has been shown, is very likely to have been the man) he is praised for many qualities. He commands a physical grace and discreet modulation of the voice. He does not reduce his speech to the prompter's hopefully audible whisper. He does not shout in a way to overcome the clash of weapons on shields. He gives music to a poet's lines. He is versatile. His chief parts seem to be in tragedy, but the named roles of Parasite and Precisian suggest capacity in satirical comedy. Precisian was a word for a Puritan at that time. To the players a Precisian was a figure for mockery, not respect.

Richard Burbage, whose family name was spelled with several variations in the second syllable, was born into the theatre, probably about 1568. His father, James, had started life as a carpenter and joiner, but 'reaping but a small lyving by the same gave it over and became a common player'. He married Ellen Brayne, the sister of a London grocer, who invested in the growing industry of play-acting in inn-yards. In 1577 they financed the erection of the first specially built play-house known as The Theatre; the site was in Shoreditch outside the jurisdiction of the play-hating City. The first price for admission was a penny. A seat in one of the three galleries cost twopence. Presumably these charges were raised when the venture became successful since there were violent quarrels over the division of the profits between the Burbages, the Braynes, and the landowner Giles Allen. They continued until the end of 1598. James had then died and his elder son Cuthbert, determined to take strong action, began to pull down the theatre and had the timber carted across the river to the South Bank where it was rapidly used as the material for the Globe and so for the most famous stage of the period.

The shares in this new and soon valuable property were divided into two sections. Cuthbert and Richard held half of them. The other half was divided into five among their leading companions in the Chamberlain's Men, Shakespeare, Heminge, Philips, Pope, and Kempe. Cuthbert never became an actor and remained their business manager. That he was popular is shown by bequests in the wills of three actors, Cowley, Tooley and Sly. Shakespeare in his will left money to Richard to buy a memorial ring as he did to Heminge and Condell, but there was nothing in word or bequest for Cuthbert. We may surmise a dispute since the other players thought of him in a friendly way. Nicholas Tooley, who died in 1623 four years after Richard Burbage, had been a lodger of Cuthbert's and was buried from their house in Shoreditch. In his will he left Cuthbert's wife ten pounds 'as a remembrance of my love in respect of her motherlie care' and made Cuthbert and Condell his executors and residuary legatees. He left ten pounds to the sister of 'my late master Richard Burbadge' and twenty-nine pounds thirteen shillings to one of Richard's eight children, the youngest daughter, Sara.

The rate of infant mortality was then appalling, and Richard and his wife Winifred suffered frequent losses. The register of their parish church, St Leonard's, recorded that eight children were baptised between 1603 and 1619. Of these five died in early childhood. The doctor and midwife in their neighbourhood may have been particularly inept since others living elsewhere with large families were not so grievously stricken or so often compelled to hear the 'surly, sullen bell', as Shakespeare called the funeral knoll, that frequent affliction of the ears in Elizabethan London. In plague-times it hardly stopped at all. From 1607 to 1609 the pestilence was at its worst and two of the young Burbages died then. Fortunately the parents escaped although there is no sign of their having a refuge in the suburbs or country as some other players did.

Burbage's death came in March, 1619, not quite three years after that of the poet and creator of his famous parts. Like Shakespeare he did not get much beyond fifty. They had lived through laborious years, and did not scorn delights, if we can judge by Shakespeare's Sonnets and the possibly authentic anecdote, left by the lawyer, John Manningham, in 1602, which told of their rivalry in an adulterous escapade. Since Shakespeare had retired from London and died in Stratford he had to wait for the flow of epitaphic praise. Burbage had it soon and in plenty and it included respect for his skill as a 'limner' along with the eulogy of his acting.

'Exit Burbage' was the testament of one who could find no words for his sense of grandeur departed. Two months after his death the Earl of Pembroke, of whose friendship with the players more will be said in the chapter called 'The Incomparables', paid his poignant tribute in the refusal of an invitation. A banquet was being given to the French Ambassador after they had seen a play. Pembroke, as Lord Chamberlain and closely attached to the King's Men, would be expected to be there. This command performance he described in a letter of apology as one 'which I being tender-hearted could not endure to see so soon after the loss of my old aquaintance Burbadg'. An elegy ascribed to John Fletcher, who succeeded Shakespeare as the principal dramatist of the King's Men, began:

> He's gone and with him what a world are dead,
> Which he revived, to be revived so,
> No more young Hamlet, old Hieronymo,
> Kind Lear, the grieved Moore, and more beside
> That lived in him, have now for ever died.

'Kind', if not a misprint for King, suggests that the author of the lines was more impressed by the broken Lear at the close than by the imperious monarch at the start and the maddened misanthrope at the climax. If so, Burbage commanded the melting mood quite as much as the eloquence of a maniac anger. Further mentioned are 'a sad lover' 'truely seen' and the compelling realism of his death scenes which, 'whilst he but seemed to bleed', caused the amazed spectators to think 'he died in deed'.

An early triumph was his *Richard III*. It was in this part that he so fascinated the wanton lady of Manningham's anecdote. The 'sad lover' suggests Romeo but there is no proof of that. Since he played the lead in *Hamlet*, *King Lear* and *Othello* it is reasonable to assume the same casting in *Macbeth* for which there is no record. About *Coriolanus* and *Antony and Cleopatra* we are left in the dark. But, since he remained 'the idol of the public', he would hardly be out of those huge parts.

His features can be seen in the painting now at Dulwich which some think to be a self-portrait. It does not bring the man to life; the mouth and chin are obscured by the moustache and beard. The forepart of the head is growing bald. There are pools of vigour in the large, dark eyes. The charm, as the author of the Character said, was in the lithe, smooth action and the controlled voice which made music of the verse without any of the bellowing of the noisier histrionics and the passion-tearing exhibitionists. Speaking Hamlet's advice to the players he was himself the exemplary follower of that counsel.

It is one of the saddest gaps in theatrical history that Shakespeare's cast-lists were not printed with the plays as they often were in the case of some other dramatists. We know from Ben Jonson that when *Every Man in his Humour* was produced in 1598, Burbage was second in the list of 'principal Comedians' which included all the pillars of the company, with Shakespeare at the head. After Burbage came Phillips, Heminge, Pope, Condell, Sly, and Kempe. In the next year Burbage was first on the comedians' list in Jonson's sequel, *Every Man Out of his Humour*.

It is lamentable that we should have no information at all about the comedy parts which he took in Shakespeare's plays. Probably these did not include Falstaff. If he had 'created' that immediately renowned role he would have had the town roaring with delight and the news would surely have spread in the gossip of which we get some echoes in letters and jotted notes of the period. The approbation would also have survived in the tributes after the player's death. Could Fletcher, who included 'old Hieronymo' in Kyd's *The Spanish Tragedy*, forget Shakespeare's greatest droll if Burbage had played it?

The length of his acting career is uncertain, since there is no record of its start which may have been as a boy player. After his death his brother Cuthbert wrote of Richard's 'thirty five years of paines, cost and labour' by which 'he made meanes to leave his wife and children some estate'. His property included land to the value of three hundred pounds and shares in the Globe and Blackfriars Theatres. These were valuable. It is known that soon after 1630 two shares in the former and three in the latter were together worth more than five hundred pounds. Richard's holdings before his death had been substantial. The mention of thirty-five years puts his entry to his father's profession in 1583.

The first appearance of his name occurs in the Plots of *Dead Man's Fortune* and *The Second Part of the Seven Deadly Sins* whose dates are put at 1591. The company presenting them was either the Admiral's or Strange's and several of the players involved joined the Chamberlain's Men after that. Of Burbage's thirty-five years twenty-five were spent as a Sharer and leading player with this company; Shakespeare is not named in the two Plots, but his link with the Chamberlain's and King's Men, until his death in 1616, was as continuous as that of Burbage. Their partnership was as unbroken as it was unsurpassed in the estimation of the Court and the play-goers.

Winifred Burbage married again and became Mrs Robinson. Her second husband was probably another Richard, the popular Dicky Robinson who had begun as a boy player with the King's Men and was named in the First Folio as one of Shakespeare's actors. The first mention of him in the records is in the cast-list of Ben Jonson's *Catiline* (1611). In that Burbage was at the head of the 'Principall Tragedians'. Dicky stayed on with the company as an adult player, probably in comedy parts, until the Civil War interrupted their work. An actor called Robinson fought on the King's side and was killed in 1645. But this must have been another man of that name since Dicky signed the dedication of the Folio of Beaumont and Fletcher plays in 1647. The register of St Anne's Church in Blackfriars records the burial of 'Richard Robinson, a player, on March 2, 1648'.

It was the custom for senior actors to take boy-apprentices into their homes as lodgers and trainees. If young Robinson had been Burbage's pupil and showed great promise with a successful career to follow that would explain Winifred's affection for him. He certainly became famous at an early age. In Ben Jonson's comedy of 1616, *The Devil is an Ass*, which was a failure distressing to its author, there is quite a long reference to Dicky. In this piece a character called Meercraft, a 'projector' or financial adventurer, wants the impersonation of a lady and that needs 'a witty boy, an excellent crack'. (Shakespeare called smart lads cracks.) When Meercraft is told that he can have a boy player the objection is raised that he will talk of the plan and 'tell the poets'. Then the projector is advised of some 'very honest lads' of whom Dicky Robinson is one, 'a very pretty fellow' who had been brought to a party dressed like a lawyer's wife.

'But to see him behave it and lay the law and carve and drink unto them and then talk bawdy and send frolics! Oh it would have burst your buttons or not left you a seam.'

Meercraft is delighted at the suggestion of this 'ingenious youth' and is assured that Dicky

'dresses himself the best, beyond forty of your very ladies. Did you never see him?'

Evidently in 1616 not to have seen Dicky Robinson and burst one's buttons was to be out of the fashion.

If Burbage had schooled him for the King's Men he was an able tutor with an apt pupil. If his widow married the clever boy later her second husband must have been much younger than she was. First mentioned in 1611, Dicky would then have been about eleven or twelve. The 'infant prodigies' began to be prodigious when mere children. According to Ben Jonson young Master Pavy had been 'three years the stage's jewel' when he died at thirteen. Winifred Burbage was a mother in 1603, possibly having married very early: she must have been at least sixteen years older than Dicky was. In the case of their marriage she was staying with her first husband's profession. The players were a cohesive company with many enemies and there was reason for keeping their talents and their money in their own society.

It is obvious that Burbage was contented with the achievements of his company and with the competence of his supporting players. Like Shakespeare he would have been most welcome elsewhere if he had chosen to go. To reach the early fifties was not to die young in the calculation of the time. Forty then marked the approach of decline; that was the view of Shakespeare in his thirties. In the plays the adjective 'old' was applied to any man with a young daughter. If Old Capulet had married only a year or two after the age appointed for Juliet's wedding he might have been thirty. The players' life at the Globe was hard on their limbs as well as their nerves. Their legs were exercised in walking from North London homes across London Bridge for a long day of rehearsal and performance. Examples of Shakespeare's sympathy with their sufferings from a failure of memory or from a sense of inferiority when sharing the stage with a popular favourite have been quoted. From 1593 onwards the creator of the part of Richard III had nothing to fear from any rival talent in his own team. But for some time there was the mighty Alleyn to outshine.

There is nothing in the tributes about his being either word-perfect or faulty in memory. He had much to memorise if he took a leading role in the fifteen new plays a year estimated to have been the company's programme when its members were working in London with no epidemic to silence them or send them on tour. One must remember too that the back-stage conditions were cramped and comfortless. Much has been calculated about the size and structure of what Shakespeare called his 'unworthy platform' and the auditorium of the Globe. Nothing is known about the size of the tiring-room. Was there a star dressing-room?

Did the senior players herd in with the Hired Men amid a flurry of quick changes and a pile of costumes? What, if any, were the water-supply and plumbing? Plainly there was very little space behind the stage and much gear to be stowed there. It would be fascinating to know more of that.

From one torment Burbage was free. He played in comedy at times, but his reputation came from tragedy in which there is less chance of an able and established actor failing badly and facing the ruin of his career. It is the clowns who collapse if they are sensitive to the feeling of the house. It is harder to win continual laughter than to sustain strong emotion in a tragedy. The Fools and jesters of all periods have had to sustain their popularity and innovate their quips and capers to suit the changing taste of a wayward audience. Shakespeare constantly thought of the crowd as fickle and he met the 'wavering multitude' in the theatre as well as in the street. To the man who must be funny, must be seen to be funny, and must be spoken of after the play as even funnier than ever, the roar of laughter is the kiss of life. When a supposedly good line misses its mark, when a jest falls with a dull thud and when the surly silence is repeated the effect can be lethal.

One thinks of Grimaldi, the darling of late Georgian London, crippled with his acrobatics and knowing that his antics and gags were beginning to create yawns instead of ecstasy. He had to retire at forty. Dan Leno, the supreme droll of late Victorian pantomime and music-hall, died insane at forty-four. In our time Tony Hancock was broken in spirit and died at forty-three. Garrick said to another actor: 'You may humbug the town for some years longer as a player of tragic parts, but comedy is a serious matter.' This is not to say that Burbage foxed his public with an adroit use of the tricks of the trade. But he was doubtless aware that it was less difficult to die nobly, reciting wonderful lines and squeezing blood from a bladder under his tunic, than to be always 'in excellent fooling' and always compelling the audience to 'burst their buttons', as Jonson put it, or 'roll in the aisles' as the 'rave notices' say now.

The player of straight parts is greatly helped by a strong or charming personality. The clown has to live on his oddity and his quirks and will soon live poorly if the public grows tired of them. What are we to make of Kempe? He was one of the three leaders and Sharers of the Chamberlain's Men at the end of 1594 when payments for Court performances at Greenwich were made to him, Shakespeare, and Burbage with no other names mentioned. He had been greeted as the successor to Tarlton, a master of drollery who had been the Queen's favourite, audacious but forgiven, and an idol of the public. He had been acclaimed as 'The jestmonger and Vice-gerent generall to the Ghost of Dicke Tarlton'. He had worked with the great Alleyn before he came to Chamberlain's. He was 'a big draw' when he arrived at the side of Shakespeare and Burbage. Yet he was the first of the renowned trio to leave.

We know that he played Peter, which is a trifle, in *Romeo and Juliet* and Dogberry in *Much Ado about Nothing* which was indeed something on which to work. Then came the separation. He quickly sold his shares in the Globe in February, 1599. A year later he began to win a wager that he would dance all the way to Norwich. What he called his 'hey-go-mad' enterprise took him a month. In February he had cold weather to keep him skipping. He immediately wrote his own account of it. *Kempe's Nine Days Wonder, Performed in a Morris from London to Norwich* was entered at Stationers' Hall on April 22. A Morris is not a solo dance. The jig was his special line.

For that kind of mingled ditty and dance he was famous. In 1598 there were allusions to it in topical satires. One of them, by E. Guilpin, said that 'Whores, beadles, bawds, and sergeants filthily chaunt Kempe's Jigge'. Bawdry and jigs went together, as Hamlet sourly observed in commenting on the taste in entertainment shown by Polonius. Kempe wrote this short and brisk account of his escapade to contradict the reports of ballad-makers who had given a false account of his itinerary. He had obviously enjoyed the crowds who had heard in advance of his coming and swarmed to meet him in the towns and villages. He was lavishly entertained and tipped by the gentry and welcomed by the Mayor of Norwich. On his return to London his dancing shoes were hung up as a memento in the Guild Hall.

It is hard to understand his rage against the 'impudent generation of ballad-makers' who had given him such advertisement; he had sought publicity and got it from them. Denouncing them as 'rascalities, beetleheads and block-heads' he also called them Shakerags. Why? The choice of that title suggests that Shakespeare's name rankled. He was next heard of as borrowing money from Henslowe who was then managing Lord Worcester's Men. Kempe was briefly employed to work with them. The money obtained by the swift turn-over of his Globe shares had gone. Dancing to Norwich was a stunt not an investment. Nothing is known of his next employment or of his death. He had previously lodged in Southwark and if he is 'the man Kempe' buried in St Saviour's Church on the South Bank in November, 1603, the end had come soon. The terse inscription was churlish. The glory had melted away.

A clown who quarrels with a successful company and the premier playwright of his time and tries to go forward on his own feet, however nimble, is taking a dangerous chance. Shakespeare had no reputation as a choleric trouble-maker; the mentions of him and the course of his career indicate the opposite. Kempe had been temperamental—to use a mild term for short-tempered—and he paid for it.

Doubtless he gagged and pressed for the laughs of the 'injudicious'. He had his grievance. Peter had been useless to him. Lancelot Gobbo, which surely must have been his assignment, gets a brief opportunity. There is no evidence that Shakespeare ever played one of his own clowns. If he had done so their parts might have been larger. He wrote better ones for Armin who followed Kempe. If *Henry V* and *Julius Caesar* were the first plays given at the Globe Kempe was not getting what he deemed to be his rights. Without a good clown's part he had only his jig at the end of the Roman tragedy. His sovereignty of the antic world was over.

Burbage had exhausting roles, but he never had to feel that he was slipping or 'out to a full disgrace'. In the Character, quoted at the beginning of this chapter and reasonably identified, he was praised for a variety of gifts and powers in prose of striking quality typical of that time when the English language was reaching the summit of its richness and vigour. It is a grievous misfortune that there was then no regular dramatic criticism. The occasional mentions of individual actors in the pamphleteers' attacks upon or defence of their profession do not provide information about distinctive methods.

Critics have made mistakes and always will. They have been pelted with vociferous abuse by their indignant victims, but they provide the material of stage-history. The print preserves the performance. What they would have said about Shakespeare we can only guess. What they would have recorded about the dates and casting of his plays and productions would have been invaluable. Moreover the style in which their reviews would have been written would have been exemplary, if we can judge by the prose in which 'An Excellent Actor' was written. It brings to the mind's eye far more of Burbage than is provided on the canvas at Dulwich.

CHAPTER VI

Enter Alleyn

❧❧

THEATRICAL CRITICISM might also have given us fascinating information about the contrast between the acting style and technique of the great rivals and protagonists of their companies, Burbage and Alleyn. Their lives ran level in age and dissimilar in their work. They were born within two years of each other. Both were described as 'bred stage-players' and both impressed the public with powers never attributed to other serious actors. The laurels were heaped on the drolls, especially Tarlton and Kempe. Edward Alleyn is first heard of with Worcester's Men in 1583 when he was nineteen. His great period came when he joined the Admiral's Men under the management of Henslowe with whom he stayed and prospered until his retirement from the stage in 1604.

He married Henslowe's daughter Joan and became very profitably associated with his father-in-law's enterprises and finance. These were widely varied. Henslowe was a miscellaneous 'projector', a dyer, a pawnbroker, and a speculator in land. Alleyn was at first chiefly concerned with his theatrical investments in the Rose Theatre, the first play-house to be built on the Southwark bank, and later in the Hope in the same area. There were richer profits away from the arts. In Southwark Alleyn had been with Henslowe a share-holder and joint 'Master of the Game' at the Bear Garden. There big money could be made and Alleyn became far wealthier than any of Shakespeare's company ever did.

Soon after the death of Henslowe's daughter in 1623 he took a second wife, Constance, the daughter of John Donne, Dean of St Paul's. It was a good match for her in a worldly way since he could afford to make her a settlement of fifteen hundred pounds. He bought land in Sussex and Yorkshire. The latter turned out to be an unlucky purchase since a journey to the North in bad weather brought on a fatal illness in 1626. His major estate was in London where he acquired the Manor of Dulwich in 1605. There he founded the College of God's Gift, endowing a Master, a Warden, four Fellows, twelve poor scholars and twelve alms-houses. Paying pupils were also taken. The College had its ups and downs but its life has been unbroken. In 1857 it was recon-stituted by a special Act of Parliament as Dulwich College and Alleyn's School. The result was excellent and the reputation for scholarship has remained extremely high. At Dulwich, whose former pupils are still called Old Alleynians, is his monument.

As an actor he was illustrious and frequently and ignorantly called the Roscius of his day. (Alleyn's famous parts were of the tragical and melodramatic kind and Roscius was the darling comedian of Rome in about 60 B.C. Yet his name lived on as a tributary title for the great strutters of the passion-tearing type. Burbage seems to have been less decorated with this flattering but ill-used label.) Alleyn's career exemplified the rise of the player in rank and responsibility. In 1610 he became a Church Warden at St Saviour's in Southwark and that office was no sinecure.

Mr G. L. Hosking in his comprehensive survey of the actor and his age, *The Life and Times of Edward Alleyn*, shows that the Warden of a parish was also a kind of magistrate with powers to fine all sorts of drinking, swearing, gambling and licentious laymen and even an incumbent who neglected his religious duties. It was not until he had retired from the stage that Alleyn took on this work in an area notorious for its tough characters. It may have appealed to him as an investment since he could legally pocket two pounds when a 'recusant' was fined twenty. Whatever his motives he had plenty to do. He had to see that dead bodies were wrapped in wool. (The wool-merchants got the law on their side to protect their industry and keep down imports of foreign fabrics.) Pre-sumably he had a sub-Warden to help him. In formal deeds he was described as 'gentleman' or yeoman. In holding parochial office while working in the theatre he was not unique. Heminge and

Condell were Church Wardens at St Mary Aldermanbury, in the City.

The description of 'musician' was used in Alleyn's case and lutes and viols were among his possessions at his death. His listed property did not include canvas, paints or paint-brushes. In their absence we cannot see him as a pictorial artist. This excludes him from the description of 'An Excellent Actor'. He left a library containing many classical and theological works, a queer product of his Bear Garden profits.

His trading in the brutalities of bull- and bear-baiting put a blot on his name for us, but more enhanced than besmirched it for his public. At that time arts and atrocities, sensitivity and savagery were queer and close companions. While of the crowds who flocked to the Globe and the Rose to hear exquisite verse some may have preferred the play to the poetry, at least they were not deterred by the beauty of the words. Yet they were the same people, headed by their play-loving Queen, who were constant visitors to the bowl of blood next door to the play-houses. Alleyn as an actor incurred the abuse of the Puritans who were more enraged by his performance on a stage than by his enrichment through cruelty to animals. A player's pretended murder was a hellish sin to them. The actual hanging of a criminal at Tyburn and the disembowelling of his still living body was a popular spectacle which they omitted to denounce. In that world of confused taste and ethics Alleyn and Burbage were the spawn of Satan to the preachers and paragons to the public. So could the former spend ten thousand pounds, with more to follow, on his Dulwich estate and enterprise. The young were served with a school, the elderly and infirm with almshouses. Burbage, with no Bear Garden revenues, left 'better than three hundred pounds'. Perhaps his widow had need to marry again.

At the beginning of the fifteen-nineties, when Lord Strange's and the Admiral's Men worked together and shared their talents, the two men seem to have been briefly colleagues. Shakespeare was then unattached and both may have appeared in one of his earliest plays. There is no record of that. No acting was allowed in London owing to the plague in 1593. When work became possible again in 1594 the teams separated and a new group was founded with royal patronage. The Chamberlain's Men set up on their own with Burbage as their leading player. Alleyn stayed with Henslowe. After that the two men began to compete for the highest praise and popularity at the head of rival companies.

Were they giving the same kind of performance with similar success or were they appealing to their audience with a markedly contrasted use of voice, gesture, and the presentation of character? Probably they were masters in different schools with Alleyn determined to be larger than life and Burbage, encouraged by Shakespeare, resolved to portray life within the modesty of nature. Hamlet's bitterly phrased contempt for the passion-tearing, ear-splitting and town-crier style of elocution must have been aimed at the men next door. The attack is driven home at length as well as in force:

O, there be players that I have seen play,—and heard others praise, and that highly,—not to speak it profanely, that, neither having the accent of Christians, nor the gait of Christian, pagan, nor man, have so strutted and bellow'd, that I have thought some of nature's journeymen had made them, and not made them well, they imitated humanity so abominably.

First Player. I hope we have reform'd that indifferently with us, sir.

Hamlet. O, reform it altogether.

There were sure to be faults of this kind to be noticed occasionally in Shakespeare's own company. The itch to 'have a bash', always endemic in high-spirited actors when the fashion allows it, was natural to Elizabethans. The men who were described by Dekker as falling upon the poets 'like swine on acorns' applied their energy to the words as well as to the glory and the money. But Shakespeare could not expect Burbage to speak the critical lines which might easily be turned against himself and his companions by a noisy, ill-mannered and scoffing member of the audience. We know that these nuisances were often there. So Hamlet's fusillade must have been aimed elsewhere. Alleyn at the Rose was the obvious target if, as its star in the ascendant, he was in blazing form. Parts in which he excelled invited him to bestride a play colossally and make his public shiver and shake. Hamlet's contemptuous remarks were aimed at one whom he 'heard others praise and that highly'. Who else was being so belauded? It is a rude onslaught, but the manners of the time did not preclude discourteous argument. The players were accustomed to reckless abuse from the dramatists who thought themselves to be getting the worst of the bargain on pay-day as much as from the railing Puritans who cried a plague on both their houses. In the exchange of verbal fisticuffs all could fight without gloves on.

We know only a few of Alleyn's famous roles. That he could be a leader in levity is shown by the entry at Stationers' Hall on January 7, 1592, of 'A comedie entitled a Knacke to knowe a knave newlye sett forth as it hath sundry times been plaid by Ned Allen and his companie with Kempe's applauded Merrymentes of the men of Goteham'. The author's name is not given. (Another snub for their profession.) The principal talents of this combination of Strange's and Admiral's Men were 'the draw'. It was most unusual to speak of an actor and 'his companie'. The team and the patron's name were nearly always given the credit on a title page. But not this time. Alleyn's presence with Kempe was a powerful attraction in comedy in the early fifteen-nineties. As Tamburlaine he had shown some years before his ability to 'ride in triumph through Persepolis', and London too. His other known victories were in Greene's *Orlando Furioso* and Marlowe's *The Jew of Malta* and *Faustus*. In the last he had a human being to present, but Tamburlaine and the Jew are monsters, not men.

If he wished to hit back at Hamlet's denigration he had effective arguments. 'A pox on your modesty of nature', he could protest, and then point out that Tamburlaine's vanity and viciousness and the Jew's glee in contriving multiple murders cannot be cut down to lifelike size. The parts must swell not shrivel in the acting. A

Furioso must live up to his name. If that meant strutting and
shouting then the feet must and would be stamped, the arms bran-
dished, and the voice sent soaring to the galleries and the sky.
For that bravura delivery Marlowe wrote: 'His words were
thunderbolts and must be hurled. And let Master Shakespeare
and his friends take note of it. The public love it. The answer is
in their hands and how they clap them! The test is in the house
and it is full.' To which Shakespeare and Burbage could reply that
they too could pack a theatre. *Hamlet* came a dozen years after
Tamburlaine, art moves on, and the theatre cannot be immobilised
in one pattern of performance.

Unfortunately the praise given to the favourite players was an
unspecified commendation. There was no recording of peculiar
methods; the effect was hailed and the ways to get it were not
examined. The writer of 'An Excellent Actor' was probably
ruling Alleyn out when he said that his ideal player 'did not strive
to make men monsters' and also stressed the refusal to drop his
voice or shout. In saying that 'by his action he fortified moral
precepts with examples' he told us nothing much. Does action
here mean acting rather than strong use of movement? It is hard
to see how that could point a moral though it might adorn a tale.
The same word is used without precise meaning in the tribute to
Alleyn in Nashe's *Pierce Penniless* (1592): 'Not Roscius nor Aesope,
those most admyred tregedians that have lived ever since before
Christ was borne, could ever perform more in action than famous
Ned Allen.' (Aesop of course is not the Greek fabulist but a
Roman tragedian and a contemporary of Roscius.) It is certain
that Alleyn, or whoever was being censured by Hamlet, put more
emphasis on action as bodily movement than Shakespeare
approved. The order not 'to saw the air too much with the hand'
is followed by the word 'thus'. That is a stage direction. Burbage
is to give a practical example of the flailing arms. If Alleyn was
notorious for his physical flourishes laughter could be expected
from those who were regular and critical play-goers and familiar
with the tricks of the trade.

As has been explained, there had to be a lot of cutting

to fit the time-scheme of the players' two (or two-and-a-half) hours traffic of the stage. The immense length of *Hamlet* made considerable omission necessary. Perhaps the speeches to the Players were not spoken. But they were kept in the 'true and perfect coppie' of the text. Shakespeare was not withdrawing.

In a small congested city with few theatres the rival companies could not live in isolation. Alleyn and Burbage had to co-operate in the ceremonies commanded for the Coronation of King James in March, 1604, but they were not side by side. The Chamberlain's Men had become the King's and their leaders were Grooms of the Chamber. They marched in new red robes with Shakespeare at their head, if we go by his priority on the list. While Burbage was one of a team Alleyn was given the honour of a solo appearance. His link with royalty had just been made by joining the new company of young Prince Henry's Men. He was commanded to impersonate the Genius of the City of London and of the Thames and to deliver a 'gratulatory speech'.

There were to be other recitals. Dekker was indignant because verses composed by Jonson, Middleton, and himself were never spoken. It was thought, perhaps correctly and tactfully, that the King had had enough. But Dekker praised Alleyn's voice and 'action' in his share of the oratory. Soon after that came the end of a stage and platform life for Alleyn. Though he was still under forty he gave up acting but kept up his financial interest in Henslowe's theatres and in the building of another play-house, the Hope, which was erected in 1613 on part of the site of the Bear Garden. The old 'game' and its profits were not forgotten. When the new house was planned the stage was made removable. Thus an arena could be substituted if plays were failing to attract and spectators of baiting were more numerous than listeners to the actors and the poets.

While Alleyn, diverse in his cultural as well as commercial interests, gave his time and money to his College and his alms-houses Burbage continued to have strenuous years in the theatre. After 1608 the King's Men had to find and hold an audience at theatres, the new, roofed-in, more comfortable and more profitable Blackfriars in addition to the Globe which was a liability in wintry weather. Burbage was a Sharer in both and had to face managerial worries while maintaining his performances, which could not be abandoned without loss since his prestige and popularity were constant. He remained a performer and he is not known to have become a projector in extraneous commercial ventures. Alleyn did not concentrate his activities. He joined Henslowe in investing in a starch-making business for which the fashions of the time, especially the ruffs, were providing a good market. The King's Men minded their own affairs and flourished well enough by their own standards of earning and living.

With Shakespeare much rusticated and soon lost altogether they had to discover and nourish new talents. As playwrights they had Francis Beaumont and John Fletcher in whose tragedy *Bonduca* Burbage was named first among the 'Principal Actors'. When Beaumont died at the early age of thirty-two in 1616 Fletcher carried on successfully as Principal Poet. Shakespeare had encouraged him with collaboration and his choice was justified by public approval of Fletcher's more romantic approach to tragedy. There was 'talent-spotting' to be done among the young entry. Dicky Robinson fulfilled all expectations. Burbage had to look for one big enough to follow himself and Joseph Taylor, of Prince Charles's Men, was the choice and a shrewd one. He followed Burbage as Hamlet and as Ferdinand in *The Duchess of Malfi* and stayed on as leading member until the Civil War. It was a challenging inheritance and well carried. Alleyn had no successor of equal eminence in his abandoned reign on the Bankside.

A sovereign position on the stage has long been and perhaps always will be held by two contrasted types of player. One has a striking and magnetic personality and is adored by his admirers who are more delighted than repelled by prominent mannerisms and idiosyncrasies of style. His devotees want him to go on being his compelling and incomparable self. To them the part is more than the play and the actor more than the part. A master of this commanding quality presents a character more than he represents it. The personal stamp is put on the dramatist's creation, often to the dramatist's advantage if he wrote for star-casting.

The other type is made victorious by his versatility and by consummate skill in altering looks, gait, and voice. Such an one does not exploit his personality but subdues it to the role. In widely different parts there is a drive through the surface of a character to its heart and essence. The first type is immediately and gladly recognised. The second sets the audience wondering whether this can really be their idol, so flexible are his methods in the use of intonation, movement, and facial expression.

There is more than sufficient evidence for Alleyn's firm grip on the public for more than a dozen years after he had stormed the theatres with Marlowe's blend of rhetoric and melodrama. There is too little information about his particular merits. It is a reasonable surmise that he imposed himself upon a part and did not seek to be natural for the very good reason that he was supplied with unnatural villains in plays of unnatural theatricality. Outsize characters must have outsize acting. Aware of his powers, he saw no reason to dwarf them. He had become the talk of the town in his early twenties and he kept it talking loudly for as long as he wanted. They could practise their realism next door because they had a dramatist who wanted it and wrote for it. The clearest case of contrasted aims is in the two Jews of Marlowe and Shakespeare. There is melodrama in Shylock's vicious attempt at revenge, but the part has attracted actors for centuries because it contains human nature as well as inhuman cruelty. There have been countless Shylocks; very few have chosen to revive Barabbas.

There is no documentary evidence that Burbage did play Shylock, but the probability is so great as to be almost a certainty. None other of the team has been mentioned. He had to give a balanced performance, winning some sympathy for the victim of savage anti-Semitism which had just been intensified by the fact that the Portuguese Jewish Doctor called Lopez had been hanged in 1594 on a charge of attempting to poison the Queen. Shakespeare's Shylock would not be a gift for Burbage in the London of

1595. Alleyn had the easier but perishable task. His Jew could 'strut and fret his hour on the stage and then be heard no more'. Burbage created the role for the centuries.

But there was a big gap in the appreciation. That it had been 'divers times acted by the Lord Chamberlain's Servants' was stated in the First Quarto of 1600. The Revels Account mentioned two performances at Court in 1603. It is astonishing to read in F. E. Halliday's *Shakespeare Companion* that there was no performance between 1605 and 1701 when it was given by Betterton in a revised form with the comedian Doggett as the Jew. But Shylock could be no joke for Burbage. If he entered into the part with perception he had as tricky a task as any that Shakespeare set him. Yet, since their co-operation continued, it is plain that Burbage played part after part as Shakespeare, speaking through Hamlet, wanted them.

The First Player at Elsinore, speaking in defence of his Company and, as the audience would take it, for the Chamberlain's Men, replies to Hamlet that some reform of their acting has been made and then is told to reform it altogether. Marlowe's chief roles for Alleyn were not of a kind for more natural acting. There is no news of his playing Edward II, a far more carefully drawn character than Tamburlaine and Barabbas and capable of natural acting. He might have resented any suggestion of 'playing it down'. Owners of the grand manner do not want to mend it or take a hint from their rivals. Both men could claim that 'one man in his time plays many parts' and both had prevailed in their own way. Alleyn remained triumphantly Alleyn while Burbage was being 'An Excellent Actor'.

CHAPTER VII

Facing the Public

❧❦❧

THE SHAKESPEARIAN actors were afternoon workers except when they were commanded to appear at a palace or a great house. The most popular could therefore be called 'matinée idols'. That term, once commonly used of London's West End stars, was applied to the well-graced who added especially good looks to good performance. At the beginning of this century, when the picture post-card industry was at its busiest, the faces of the favourites, costing a penny plain and twopence glossy, were widely on sale in all kinds of shops among the newspapers, sweets and cigarettes.

As a boyhood fancier I collected the darlings of the day, Zena and Phyllis Dare, Lily Elsie, Gabrielle Ray, and other bright shiners in the musical comedies and the music-halls. They were 'pin-ups' on the walls and 'paste-ups' in albums. The Shakespearians were sometimes leaders in the masculine market, being handsome as well as excellent in the quality they professed: Lewis Waller had been impressively heroic as Henry V, Forbes-Robertson nobly and austerely beautiful as Hamlet, and George Alexander, as Orlando, had passed the usually devastating criticism of Bernard Shaw who surprisingly said that he would like to see this performance again. A setter of literary competitions might ask for a mimic Shavian notice of Burbage as Hamlet and Shakespeare as the Ghost. How caustic would G.B.S. have been? At least he could not have dismissed them as matinée idols.

In the picture post-card epoch there were no films or television and most of the post-card buyers went rarely, if at all, to the London theatre. The portraiture was liked for decorative reasons. To the public the world of the theatre was remote, mysterious, and romantic. Its personalities, if ladies, had to be 'pretty as a

Edward Alleyn

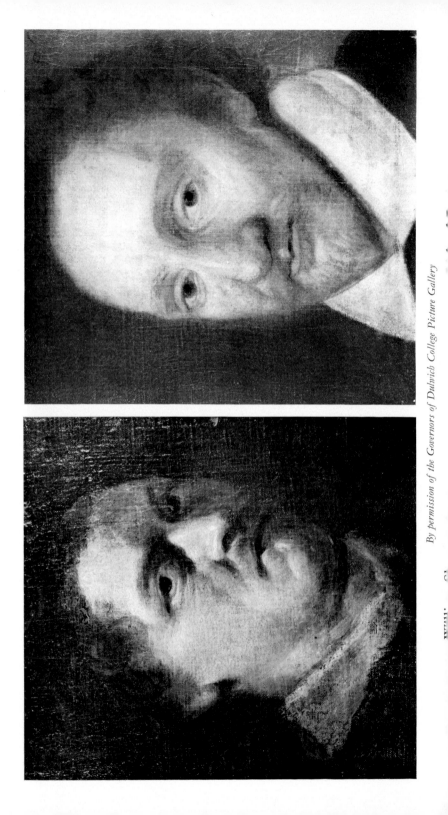

By permission of the Governors of Dulwich College Picture Gallery

picture' and, if men, photogenic with the appropriate features of a beau. Then came the cinema and the faces that launched a thousand films.

To bring us face to face with the original Shakespearian actors we have some portraiture of a mediocre kind and of limited range. The artists are unknown. Only the seniors are on view. We have no picture of the children or lads who had to 'boy the greatness' of a Cleopatra or the golden beauty of a Portia. The leading men of Shakespeare's company were never painted in their famous parts. A rather drab realism keeps romance at a distance. Elizabethan portraiture at its best was concentrated on royalty and the nobility and in their case it profited by the finery of their clothes and jewels. They had their vanity: they loved display and they dressed to create the image of a sumptuous elegance.

The actors did not have the service of the chief artists. There was no attempt at idolising. They were presented without benefit of stage costume and for some reason were apt to appear before the easel in curiously sombre attire. Most surprisingly gloomy is the full-length Alleyn. With his broad-brimmed and crowned hat, his ample beard, moustache and whiskers, and his long, dark gown, relieved only by a white ruff, he appears completely untheatrical. This sober-suited citizen may well be the pious founder of 'the College of God's Gift'. He is leagues away from the young man who stormed the town as Tamburlaine. At least so he seems now.

The engraving of Shakespeare's head and shoulders by Martin Droeshout, who was only thirteen when Shakespeare died, is supposed to have been made from a line drawing by an unknown artist. That it provides at least a formal resemblance is indicated by its acceptance by Heminge and Condell for the First Folio. If so, it is a kind of likeness without any kind of life. One cannot think of Shakespeare without animation. The first engraving was later touched up with slight additions to the light moustache and the hair below the lower lip. The cheeks have more hints of an incipient beard. The tall brow and bald scalp are doubtless accurate, but for the rest one cannot see truth to the lively man in anything so dull. Was the owner of these features ever gay or ever sad? Was he ever an actor?

It can be replied that those who look for what is called 'an actor's face', something like the powerful image of Sir Henry Irving, will get no satisfaction from what we see of Shakespeare's colleagues. Burbage, whether or not he was his own artist, has a long nose, a heavy moustache, and a trim but rather deterrent beard. The eyes are large, dark, and vivid. They could 'look daggers', no doubt, but a bearded player works under handicap. Few, if any, actors of our or recent times have thus lumbered themselves. Nobody today expects to meet an Olivier or a Gielgud in the street so facially obscured.

The woodcuts of the clowns, Tarlton of the Queen's Men and Kempe of the Chamberlain's, show them bearded. The other members of Shakespeare's 'fellowship' of whom we have portraits are seen unbearded. John Lowin, who joined them in 1603, is shown with a moustache and small imperial. If that was his accustomed look he must have made up for Falstaff and Henry VIII in which roles he was said to excel. William Sly, an early member of the team, was a heavily built man with a slight moustache. The lissom Nathan Field, a late recruit, presents the liveliest appearance. He had the reputation of being a 'lady's man' and looks the part with his slight, dark moustache and little 'imperial' chin-tuft.

No dingy doublet for him. He is dressed to attract, evidently aware, as the others are not, that a player who sits for a portrait should make an effort for the occasion. He may be wearing a stage-costume. His right hand is on his heart. Was that a routine of theatrical portraiture? It is curious that the three actors whose arms are shown, Alleyn, Lowin, and Field, are posed in this way, but Alleyn's hand, not reaching as far to his left, is settled on his diaphragm, suggesting more heart-burn than heart-felt emotion. That wise and practical Shakespearian director, W. Bridges-Adams, oddly discovered an explosive power in the Alleyn portrait. I can only see in this gesture the menace of dyspepsia.

The character called Gullio in the second of the Cambridge

'Parnassus' plays is a Shakespearian devotee. This enraptured scholar says that he will keep the author's *Venus and Adonis* under his pillow and 'have his picture' in his study. This suggests that there was a 'pin-up' cult in or around 1600, but we can only guess what sort of picture was available for the collectors. The compliment is paid to 'Sweet Mr Shakespeare' the poet whom he puts well ahead of Spenser and Chaucer. Shakespeare the player is not mentioned. Perhaps Gullio, an avid reader, had never seen or heard of him 'in the motley'. But the epics and the plays had made him eager to see the creator of such dulcet lines. The great tragedies were yet to come. Shakespeare to his admirers was, in the words of Francis Meres, 'mellifluous and honey-tongued'.

The contemporary praise of the actors by the addicts of the theatre centres on their voices, their vivacity, and their realistic simulation of a humour or a passion. The anonymous description of 'An Excellent Actor', already quoted, likens him to 'a grave orator'. It extols his 'full and significant action', his speech well tempered to the moods of a part, and his ability to add music to a poet's 'ditty'. There is no allusion to commanding features or the enchantment of a superlatively handsome face. The principal appeal came by way of the ear and mind. If the players' admirers were then more drawn by compelling performance than by the façade of a 'matinée idol' they showed their appreciation of the essentials.

The foppish notables of the courtier class were usually moustached and bearded. Their portraits indicate attention to their trimming. The players who took such parts were equipped for them if they were not clean-shaven. Hamlet alludes to his own beard and a few modern actors have presented him thus 'vallanced'. But concealment of the mouth is a hindrance and the most notable Hamlets have chosen to keep him shaven, not because they wanted to be 'matinée idols' but because an uncluttered mouth and face provide more scope for recording thought and feeling with subtle varieties of expression. Sir John Gielgud and the Hamlets whom I have most admired would have been sadly hampered without the visible freedom of their lips. Had they appeared in Elsinore otherwise, I for one should have repeated the Prince's advice, 'It shall to the barber's'. For many Shakespearian roles the actor who uses a razor may be unhistorical but is more theatrical.

The costumes worn in performance were strangely assorted. Sometimes money was lavishly spent on them. Henslowe, certainly no wastrel, paid the then enormous sum of twenty pounds for a copper-lace robe for Alleyn. But the sumptuous appearance could be gained without great expense. The milords and miladies with rich wardrobes gave their superfluity to their servants who sold them to the actors. Thus a bedizened dandy on the stage could dress the part without driving his company's treasurer to distraction. But a troupe having hard times could not cope with display. On tour with a wagon there must have been strict limitation of properties and panoply.

Historical accuracy in the mounting of a Shakespearian play was not attempted until the middle and end of the nineteenth century. Then the costs of a lavish production were low and could be recovered during the run of a play. In addition to a full spread of canvas and huge stage-crowds the antiquaries worked to provide accuracy in heraldry and costume. The Elizabethan players could expect only a few performances for each new venture and could not possibly risk their meagre capital on any one play. When they chose garments these had to be available for a number of plays set in widely varying countries and periods. The cloak that covered a Roman emperor on one day was adorning a Renaissance courtier on the next. The money was limited; so was space in the tiring-room.

For a classical play there might be some vaguely Greek or Roman attire ready to hand. If that did not suffice Elizabethan outfits were included. This is clearly shown by the drawing of a scene from *Titus Andronicus* endorsed 'Henrye Peacham's Hande, 1595'. Queen Tamora is pleading with Titus to spare her sons. They appear in sketchily 'period' dress, but the two guards wear the breeches and doublets of Elizabethan sentries. Neither actor nor spectators would worry about this contrast. The dramatic impact was all that mattered and here one gory deed came pat upon another. If the blood flowed who cared what kind of costume it soaked? The play in this case was crude. But in a tragedy of supreme grandeur there was still no realism in the apparel. Cleopatra's laced stomacher, impossible on the Nile in 33 B.C., was acceptable on the Bankside of the Thames in A.D. 1608.

In the part of a medieval nobleman the actor would be expected to look as splendid as might be. The wealthier members of the audience were dandies and could not accept a supposed grandee who looked shabby on the stage. But the picture was less than the poetry and the passion. Rehearsals were not interrupted, as they are now, for a long series of shots in front of a camera. The player was there to make the most of his lines, thundering, tender, or witty. He was the music-maker of the poet's 'ditty' and not the exhibit of a director more interested in visual effects than in the purpose of the play. When he was facing a portrait-painter he chose to be his serious self. He was not posing and smiling to the satisfaction of a Press Agent, expert in the promotion of personalities.

CHAPTER VIII

The Boys

꽃꽃ꩳ

Through the mouth of Rosencrantz Shakespeare complained about 'the little eyases' (young hawks) who so berattled the common stages as to be 'most tyranically clapped for't'. The choice of adjective suggests quite a deep resentment. The young squawkers in a near-by nest were getting a bit above themselves, as tyrants do, winning larger audiences and more applause than their seniors liked. That was a nasty fact to be noted when the men at the doors were handing over the money in their boxes for manager Heminge to count, perhaps with Shakespeare looking anxiously over his shoulder. The Chamberlain's Men were doing well but they were aware of strong competition. So it seems to be clearly hinted.

The Children's Companies were plentiful rivals. There is record of eleven such teams in the contested field at various times after Elizabeth became Queen and encouraged them, but it is not certain that they were all only or mainly acting since the primary recruitment was for singing in church. Recruitment perhaps understates the vigour with which a good treble voice was sought for and enrolled. Three years after her succession in 1558 the Queen commanded a nation-wide hunt and did so in strong terms.

'For that it is meet that our chapel royal should be furnished with well-singing children from time to time we have and by these presents do authorise our well-beloved servant Richard Edwardes, master of our children of our royal chapel, or his deputy, to take as many well singing children as he ... shall think meet in all cathedral and collegiate churches ... within this realm of England.'

In 1585 Thomas Giles, the Master of the Cathedral Church of St Paul, was authorised to 'bring away without any lets, contradictions, stay, or interruption' anywhere in England and Wales children 'fit to be instructed and framed in the art and science of music and singing'. This talk of taking and bringing away almost suggests a press gang. The youngsters may have been delighted at this removal to the excitements of London. But what did the parents think and what security was there for the morals of the lads? If they heard the voice of the Puritans denouncing the actors as 'Schoolmasters of Bawdry and idleness' and worse they had cause for apprehension. But families were large. Here at least was one brat out of the way and on his way to earn a living.

Out of the choirs came the emerging and soon very popular boy actors. Their talents were rapidly in demand. Between 1558 and 1576, that is before James Burbage opened his London Theatre for adult professionals (with children soon assisting in the women's parts) the Court commanded more performances from juvenile troupes than it did from senior strolling players (forty-six as opposed to thirty-two). The development of dramatic work by the mature actors after the opening of Burbage's house diminished the favour shown to the Children's Companies, but in 1600, when *Hamlet* was being written, the competition was being renewed and the tyrannical applause was being won by the St Paul's boys who offered new plays by established dramatists.

There was even stronger rivalry to come from the Children of the Chapel Royal who were established in rooms at the Blackfriars Priory which James Burbage had converted into a theatre. It seems that the elder Burbage by adapting these premises had caused trouble for the future. But it was his son, the great Richard, who made a serious mistake by rashly leasing this Blackfriars Theatre to Giles and Evans who were in management with the Children of the Chapel as their principal asset. Moreover they had Jonson as one of their dramatists, not as powerful an attraction as Shakespeare, it is true, but a coming man whose vigorous and quarrelsome personality kept him in the news.

There was trouble. Giles was attacked on two grounds. He

was charged with collecting boys with no musical talent and putting them to 'the base trade of mercenary player'. Worse still, the son of an important father, Sir Henry Clifton, had been kidnapped with 'great force and violence' and committed to the Blackfriars play-house to work with 'lewd and dissolute players'. Sir Henry carried this accusation to the Queen and the boy was released. A halt to the enterprise was ordered. But soon the irrepressible boys were back again and actually with a royal title as 'The Children to the Revels of the Queen'.

Fortunately for Burbage, Shakespeare, and the King's Men Giles made another serious blunder by producing in 1605 *Eastward Ho*, a comedy in which Jonson, Marston, and Chapman collaborated and were stupid enough to include jokes against the Scots. The King, who was still James VI of Scotland as well as James I of England, was not amused. Indeed he was so little pleased that two of the dramatists had a taste of prison life. The Children themselves had not offended, but their progress was checked.

The King's Men had their revenge for past annoyances when in 1608 they took over the Blackfriars Theatre for themselves and found it to be more profitable than the Globe. Giles had been ordered to see that choirboys stayed in their proper place, the Cathedral, since it was 'not fit or decent' that those chosen 'to sing the praise of God' should be trained and employed in 'lascivious and profane exercises'. The King's Men were victorious over their rivals for a while and also had the satisfaction of recruiting some valuable talent from them. Field, Underwood, and Ostler, all mentioned in the cast-list in the First Folio, had been trained as Children of the Chapel.

There is no evidence that Shakespeare ever provided a play specially for a Children's Company. He wrote long and rewarding feminine parts for boys, but he evidently decided that while boys could be excellent girls they were 'o'er-parted' as men. Other dramatists, including John Webster, in addition to those mentioned, could not afford to stay out when the young were providing so good a market for the needy playwright who lacked

Shakespeare's assured position. In 1598 Jonson, who was eight years younger than Shakespeare, was working his way up when Shakespeare was at the top and he was always short of money. So the Children were very useful to him.

No more need be said in general about the Children's Companies since their chronicles have been fully related and documented by Sir Edmund Chambers in his four volumes on *The Elizabethan Stage* and by other well-equipped scholars since then. What concerns a study of Shakespeare in the theatre is his attitude to and employment of boy actors. It is noticeable that neither Rosencrantz nor Hamlet suggests their incompetence on the stage or decries their behaviour on or off it. There is some discussion of current theatrical contentions which are causing 'much throwing about of brains' and it is agreed that the 'boys carry it away'.

Hamlet salutes a young actor who has grown a beard and so has finished with feminine roles and then he greets his successor in these parts with the kindly hope that he will not grow too tall or lose the childish voice. When the young man has given an example of his diction and delivery as Hecuba he is told 'Tis well'. In this series of 'theatre shop' discussions, absurdly irrelevant to Hamlet and his personal and political Danish problems, but fascinating to students of stage history, the criticism is directed at those members of the public who had been preferring the infant prodigy to the fully trained and capable adult. Not a word is said which could be resented by the boy who is playing Ophelia.

Who took the parts of older women, such as Gertrude, is one of the unsolved questions. Was it a grown man of an effeminate kind who shaved if necessary or a versatile boy who could be cast as a mother when he had grown too big for a child's part? Ophelia would certainly be given to the leading boy of the company and he could not be embarrassed by any remark of Hamlet's. Shakespeare had been extremely churlish about the posturing ranters in a rival house. Only on one occasion does he use an unkind adjective about the player of a woman's part.

A puzzling remark is that made by Cleopatra when she is

determined to cheat Octavius Caesar of his triumph. Antony is dead. Her position is hopeless. She foresees the humiliation of the triumph in Rome.

> Saucy lictors
> *Will catch at us, like strumpets; and scald rimers*
> *Ballad us out o' tune: the quick comedians*
> *Extemporally will stage us, and present*
> *Our Alexandrian revels; Antony*
> *Shall be brought drunken forth, and I shall see*
> *Some squeaking Cleopatra boy my greatness*
> *I' the posture of a whore.*
>
> (*Antony and Cleopatra*, V, ii.)

Is the boy player of Cleopatra's enormous role chancing a laugh and the comment from some sardonic wit with his sixpenny seat on the stage, 'Squeaker! That's you'? The last act of this tremendous tragedy is calling for a supreme performance and Shakespeare was driving on in a fast fury of inspiration. It was careless on his part to risk the line about a squeaker. But it cannot have been meant cruelly when it was written since for all he knew his Cleopatra might be making the hit of a lifetime. Cleopatra might well have been played by a not too masculine man, possibly by him who had recently been Goneril or Regan and was accustomed to the mature women's parts. Cleopatra in 31 B.C. had had her years with Julius Caesar and borne him a son. She was in Rome when he was murdered thirteen years earlier. At the time of her death she was thirty-nine. It was a tough part for a boy with an unbroken voice. Whoever was cast the opportunity was immense.

What happened to this masterpiece is a mystery. *The Booke of Antony and Cleopatra* was entered by a bookseller called Edward Blount at Stationers' Hall in May, 1608. He also entered *The Booke of Pericles, Prince of Tyre* at the same time. Blount was obviously a devotee of Shakespeare since he became one of a group who guaranteed the expense of printing the First Folio. Yet he did not mention the name of the author in making the entries and no Quarto of *Antony and Cleopatra* appeared. *Pericles*

was printed in a bad text by Henry Gosson in the following year
with an attribution to Shakespeare alone, which was incorrect
since it is obviously a piece shared with another and inferior
hand. That it was insufficiently Shakespearian was the opinion of
Heminge and Condell who omitted it from the First Folio.
Pericles was described on the title page of its Quarto as 'divers
and sundry times acted by His Majesties Servants at the Globe
on the Banck-side'.

Pericles was a conspicuous success. Reprinting was frequent
and continued until the Sixth Quarto appeared in 1635. No
Quarto of *Antony and Cleopatra* emerged and no impact on the
public was noted. 'No record of a seventeenth-century production'
is all that Halliday, among the records of performances in his
comprehensive and reliable *Shakespeare Companion*, could find to
say of it. Meanwhile *Pericles* was adding steadily to its good reception at the Globe where it was still in the repertory of the King's
Men in 1631. It was royally commanded at Court to entertain
distinguished French visitors in 1619. It did not make too heavy
a demand on a boy player. In Marina, defending her innocence,
there is a charming part, neither too long nor too difficult for a
lad of fourteen.

This success drew a sneer from Ben Jonson in his vituperative
poem of retirement beginning 'Come leave the loathed stage'.
The public, he snarled, had rejected his lusty wine and with its
swinish taste was swallowing the lees of the drama including
'Some mouldy tale like Pericles'. Jonson had been rebuffed by
the failure of his later work, but Shakespeare had had his own
set-back. While the mouldy *Pericles*, only his in part, continued
to be played and applauded both his *Coriolanus* and his *Antony
and Cleopatra* remained unprinted in Quarto and with no recorded
performance. The first that we hear of *Coriolanus* is of an adaptation by Nahum Tate for Drury Lane in 1682. We owe their
rescue from oblivion to Heminge and Condell, possibly urged by
Blount to be sure of including them while they were leaving out
Pericles. Both must have had a fair chance on the stage. Shakespeare, with *Macbeth* and *King Lear* only a year or two behind him,

was far from being finished and compelled to expect diminished popularity. That *Coriolanus* misfired is understandable. It has never been a favourite with the theatre public nor has it been ranked high by readers. It lacks the compulsion of high tragedy and of Shakespeare at his best. But the failure of *Antony and Cleopatra* demands explanation and the reasons for it are of particular interest to me because I find so much of it to merit the adjective which Charmian gave her mistress, unparalleled.

Is failure too strong a word? The absence of a Quarto after the book had been entered is strange. So is the lack of appearance in the list of Command Performances. King James was not averse to tragedy. He had ordered *King Lear* and could not have done so in ignorance of its contents since plays were never requested at Court without some public performance. None of the foreign visitors or recorders of public affairs including plays said anything about it. Antony was never mentioned as one of Burbage's great achievements. It is a magnificent role with its picture of the great lover possessed by a soaring and frustrated ambition. There are the reckless generosity, the wild gambling in the casino of world power, and the courage in defeat. No less rich in opportunity was the role of Cleopatra, the most exacting and, if the challenge can be met, the most rewarding feminine part that Shakespeare ever wrote for a boy.

The company may have complained that here was too big an order for their numbers and capacities. In its wanderings across the Italian and Near Eastern world the play contains thirty-one speaking characters. (*Hamlet* has twenty-four, *Macbeth* twenty-six and *King Lear* twenty.) In addition to the speaking parts which needed doubling and trebling in the customary manner there are 'Officers, Soldiers, Messengers, and other Assistants', some with a line or two to say. Rehearsals would have been hard labour. The chaos in the tiring-room must have been appalling. That kind of demand on limited resources had been met before but never to such a burdensome degree. If we assume that the effort was made what went wrong? Confusion on the stage or collapse in the acting?

Burbage was unlikely to fail or even falter. He was at the height of his power, widely experienced and had no cause to be apprehensive. He was about forty, just right for Antony who died at fifty-two. Cleopatra on the other hand was a colossal task for a boy or a young man if such an one was preferred for a part in which there are such rapid and violent alterations of mood from infatuation to passion and from the antics of the frisking play-girl to the despair of an imperious and thwarted queen. Enobarbus proclaims her infinite variety and the tremendous force of her emotions. 'We cannot call her winds and waters sighs and tears; they are greater storms and tempests than almanacs can report.'

She is savage and sadistic in her rage on receiving bad news. To Antony she is both treacherous and loyal, his treasure and his torment. She must rise to a peak of cool gallantry in her death. Shakespeare asked much of Juliet, far more of Cleopatra. Poor boy who must be both charmer and chameleon, sharp of tongue, short of temper, a skittish wanton and a 'regular, royal Queen'! All this and a speaker of superb poetry. If he had nervous spasms, felt o'er-parted by Burbage and was 'put beside his part' his dramatist could not fairly curse the youngster.

Robertson Davies has considered the Cleopatra problem in an excellent but, I think, neglected book, *Shakespeare's Boy Actors*. That author has the advantage of being an actor and playwright as well as a scholar, yet he overlooks the difficulties. He is not puzzled as I am. The part, he decides, is 'well within the technical and emotional scope of a boy actor of sixteen or seventeen. . . . In presenting Cleopatra the boy actor would show her primarily as a queen with a queen's dignity.' He admits that the levity and pettishness must be worked in by the player who would also tone down the voluptuousness and present 'an enchantment far above mere sensual charm'. I cannot see it so. Mr Davies admits that 'a small boy could not play the role without seeming ridiculous'. That is agreed. But could any male 'teenager' handle it in a way to combine the ugly fury and lust with the 'finest parts of pure love' for which Enobarbus has told the audience to look? At the beginning of the play Shakespeare is cruelly explicit about what the audience can expect.

If the play did not attract and was even a disaster it may be that the boy botched his part, but he could fairly have blamed the author for the enormity of his job. To add to the part's difficulty is its length. No other of Shakespeare's women has to face so continuous a strain. In the first scene of Act I Cleopatra takes the stage with Antony after thirteen explanatory lines have been spoken. She dies only shortly before the end of Act V. Antony has died at the end of Act IV. She has a whole act to carry without him. And throughout the play she has been constantly engaged. She is not dressed for the Egyptian climate. Thus there was the added labour of wearing the bulky splendour of a royal lady of the Jacobean Court. 'Cut my lace, Charmian,' she cries in distress. She was tightly encased. It was too much for too long, glorious for us to read but for a boy impossible. If intended for a young man it was still a dazzling and a baffling challenge.

In his interesting record called *Drag* of female impersonation down the ages, Mr Roger Baker includes the belief that Robert Gough or Goffe was both the first Juliet and the first Cleopatra. There is no contemporary evidence for this and Mr Baker is only mentioning it as a guess. The exact dates of the first productions of both plays are uncertain, but the usual dating puts ten or perhaps a dozen years between them. Mr Baker suggests that if the boy had gone on specialising in women's roles he must have become so expert that Shakespeare was confident that 'his most womanly creation would be safe in his hands'. If so, he was probably far too sanguine. So the play's history (or sad lack of history) suggests.

Shakespeare had not asked for as much before and prudently took care not to ask for it again. His younger women were henceforward to be what used to be called 'ingénue parts'. Perdita and Miranda were no burden to the boys. Imogen is a model of innocence and becomes one of the 'breeches parts' in which a boy scored easily. The married or elder women, Hermione and Paulina, are supporting roles. Henry VIII's Queen Catherine

has her big scenes, compelling speeches, and poignant ending at
Kimbolton. Her appearances are important but not continually
recurrent as Cleopatra's are. The men must carry the play. A
dramatist who knew his craft and his company had for once
blundered. Because he was entranced by Cleopatra he created a
part which only a highly gifted actress can play. In the great
comedies written between 1598 and 1600 he had written witty,
scintillating roles for a boy or succession of boys whom he could
trust, but they were not required to be infinitely various.

The audience took for granted the routine appearance of boys
in girls' roles. The period dresses worn by them when not in
'the breeches parts' of which Shakespeare was fond were more
than ample covering and did not invite amorous contact apart
from kissing of the hand or lips. Nothing could have been further
from the nudity recently to be seen in the plays and films which
are described as 'with it' and are in regard to costume very much
without it. If the spectators were of a kind to be embarrassed by
the sight of a man and a boy making love Shakespeare did little
to worry them. The passion was in the poetry. If that were spoken
with conviction there was no need and no request for prolonging
the lover's words with the long and lavish embraces now familiar.
Antony and Cleopatra is a notable example of speech that is aflame
with desire while the action is left to the imagination. 'My bluest
veins to kiss', says Cleopatra extending a seemingly white hand.
That she had been pictured as 'with Phoebus' amorous pinches
black' was an error since the Ptolemies were Greeks not Africans.
Had Shakespeare had a woman of his own in mind, perhaps a
haunting memory of the dark-haired, white-skinned lady of the
Sonnets? However that may be, the boy actor probably did more
than smirch his face with umber, as Rosalind did for her Arden
escapade, and was made up with a strong dark colouring to
justify the line already quoted.

It was not part of the Puritan indictment that the play-goers
were debauched with the sight of nudity. Cleopatra's demand for
a slackening of her stomacher shows how far she was from doing a
strip-tease act. The fashions of the ladies at Court exposed the

neck; below that all was concealed, and there was surprise when Queen Anne appeared as a goddess in a Court Masque wearing a skirt 'not much below the knee'. This caused one commentator to remark, 'We might see that a woman had both feet and legs which I never knew before.' Boys as women on the stage concealed the fact of bifurcation so far as to possess no visible ankles.

The Shakespeare Concordance includes two long and closely printed columns of the lines in which kisses and kissing are cited, but many of these refer to courtly or formal salutes and the putting of lips to a royal or loved one's hand. A kiss can be a slight acknowledgement of friendship, social not sexual, as it has become with many people in our time. There was the old word buss for a more lusty and possibly lustful contact. 'We buss our wantons and our wives we kiss', wrote Parson Herrick in one of his less clerical moods. Shakespeare knew the word, but used it only four times. Only on one occasion did he apply it to the wanton. Falstaff says to Doll Tearsheet that she gives him 'flattering busses'. Otherwise it is used metaphorically. The towers of Troy were said to 'buss the clouds', a cool and metaphorical embrace.

Shakespeare asked the player of Doll, whose part is not one for a small boy, to display some show of lechery in her fondling of Falstaff, but such happenings are unusual. In *Troilus and Cressida* (IV, iv), Cressida, when she has deserted Troilus and Troy, is kissed by four Greek notables in turn but one of them, Nestor, is senile. They have been enjoying a buss and certainly she was a teasing minx since Ulysses describes the seductive methods of this 'daughter of the game' in detail.

> *There's language in her eye, her cheek, her lip,*
> *Nay, her foot speaks; her wanton spirits look out*
> *At every joint and motive of her body.*

Those who impersonated light or lascivious women had to use the kind of eye once known as 'glad' for which type of beckoning Shakespeare had his own queer Frenchified term, oeillades. These, together with 'most speaking looks', were at Goneril's command. Granville-Barker, unlikely to be wrong in any matter of Shakes-

ÆTAT. 64.
Aº 1640.

John Lowin

Reproduced from the original among the Harley Papers at Longleat, by permission of the Marquess of Bath pearian direction, decided that 'the cruder phases of the emotional traffic between male and female' were not employed. But the Puritans did not agree. Their hatred of a sensual exhibition was, however, stated in general terms. Individual examples were not specified. One wonders whether the makers of these vehement attacks ever ventured to enter the sinful premises and see for themselves. Their scolding must have been based on hearsay.

Stubbs said that on scandalous view there were 'kissing and bussing, clipping and culling, winking and glancing of wanton eyes'. The most explicit denunciation of outrageous spectacle came from Prynne who alleged 'lewde adulterous kisses and embracements . . . Whorish, lust-inflaming sollicitations . . .' and 'reall lively representations of the act of venery which attend and set out stage playes'. But Prynne was writing sixteen years after Shakespeare's death. The theatre may have become more permissive when he heard about, if he did not see, these 'Brothel-house obscenities'.

The accusations of sodomy, which Stubbs had made long before Prynne plied his scourging pen, are also part, but a quite small part, of a general fury. The main brunt of the attack was on the stimulation of heterosexual misconduct. There must have been some cause for homosexual inclinations and intrigues in a masculine world where good-looking and precocious owners of treble voices were playing the parts of the charming or seductive women. Yet the Puritan assault was concentrated on the incitement to normal sexual indulgence. The exceptions were few. Stubbs charged the actors with sodomy in their 'secret conclaves', which he cannot have attended, and Prynne included the 'unnatural Sodomitical sinne of uncleanesse' in his catalogue of the play-house abominations. It is remarkable that there is no news of scandal in the theatres and no boy or company of boys was ever singled out as guilty. In the reign of King James the subject was better left alone since his Queen did not monopolise his affections and the habits of his favourites were notorious. Stubbs was railing against sodomy before James came to the throne and Prynne did so after his death.

The actors who took the boy apprentices into their homes for training were married men with families, often large ones. There can be no idea of a dissolute, Bohemian, hard-drinking life which was likely to corrupt their young entry. They were too busy for that. They were thrifty as their wills prove and they could not become Church Wardens without a solid reputation for an orderly life. Many of the boys climbed or were propelled up the ladder of their careers to mature as capable players of the senior parts. The general picture of a happy as well as efficient schooling in their life-work is sustained by a letter to Mistress Alleyn which Alleyn wrote for his pupil, Master Pyk, while they were on tour. The handwriting is that of the man, the sentiments those of the boy who sent good wishes to all at home, including the servants, from 'Your petty, pretty, prattling, parleying Pig'. He was quite the young gentleman and far from being a serf who had to be useful about the house. He greeted a servant called Sara who cleaned his shoes and another called Dolly who woke him in the morning. If these two had used the lingo of the maids in a Victorian nursery they might have called him a little jockey or a perfect caution. He worked with Alleyn for Lord Strange's Men in 1593 and for the Admiral's four years later. No more is known of his career.

The training was exacting. A writer of a book called *The Rich Cabinet furnished with varietie of excellent descriptions*, which was printed in 1616, laid down the requisites for a capable actor. They included dancing, activity, music, singing, elocution, a good memory, skill in handling weapons and 'pregnancy of wit'. To graduate in that school meant application and readiness for discipline. The boy actors who were enlisted or conscripted as choristers and then absorbed into the special Children's Companies to play all sorts of parts were in a different class from those apprenticed to senior members of the Men's Companies in order to take the feminine roles. Thus the player of Ophelia for the Chamberlain's Men may have resented the competition of the little 'eyases' as much as Hamlet did. But in one respect the two classes of juvenile performers were alike. They were not cosseted with flattery and public attention. They did not get the publicity and could not get the photography now heaped on young actresses who are thus hoisted on their way up.

In the contemporary writing about the theatre by the pamphleteers and composers of tributary verses there was frequent reference by name to the great men of high tragedy, Alleyn and Burbage, and to the masters of low comedy, Tarlton and Kempe. There was no glorification of the boys. We hear of Master Pyk only through the accidental preservation of a private letter. Jonson wrote his moving farewell to Master Pavy, but the short-lived lad was not there to know of it. A kindly obituary notice gratifies the relatives, not the subject. Of individual boys we hear almost nothing. The exception is the precocious Dicky Robinson whose amusing female impersonations were praised by Jonson. No painted portrait of a boy actor is known.

If there had been newspapers with gossip columns, picture pages, and theatre news written up from the handouts of Press Agents the atmosphere would have been totally different and far less healthy for the boys. They had no idea of being headline personalities and that saved them from swollen heads and from jealous resentments if one got more puffing than another. The pupils were not encouraged to think themselves more important than their masters.

The cast-list in the First Folio includes several men who began as boys in Shakespeare's company. Samuel Gilburne had evidently been a favourite pupil of Augustine Phillips who died in 1605 and left 'my late apprentice' forty shillings, his mouse-coloured velvet hose, his white taffety doublet, his black taffety suit, his purple cloak, his sword, dagger, and bass viol. This former pupil was well set up as a senior player and a foppish man about the play-house. We need not suspect an infatuation. Phillips was not a homosexual bachelor: he had a wife and four daughters to provide for and property to leave them. He had done well as a Sharer, having a suburban home and some land at Mortlake. Shakespeare headed the list of his minor legatees, all members of the company, who received sums of thirty or twenty shillings. Gilburne had the largest gift of money and perhaps needed it since we know nothing of his career as an adult. The will is pleasantly typical of others which reveal the friendships between the elders and their trainees.

The last name on the Folio list is that of John Rice who was apprenticed to Heminge in 1607 and may therefore have played some of Shakespeare's important feminine parts. He left the King's Men for a while, rejoined them, and then left them again to become a clergyman in Southwark at the players' parish church. That was one better than being a Church Warden. In 1630 he was a beneficiary and overseer of Heminge's will in which he was described as a 'loving friend'. Dr Johnson said that epitaphic remarks are not made on oath, but the last bequests and testaments of the players are so full of friendliness that a notion of cordial relation long continued is natural and probably justified.

Things were not so happy in the rival school of talent. Henslowe, who traded in talent, noted in his Diary that he 'bought' a boy, James Bristow, and hired him to his own team, the Admiral's Men, for three shillings a week. It is not recorded that any actor left Henslowe anything. Having died in 1616 he could not appear in the will of Alleyn whom he had helped to become wealthy. Alleyn remembered his family and was very bountiful to his charities. He did not think of his fellow-actors or his old trainees such as the prattling Pyk. The professional and clannish loyalty of the King's Men was unique.

The history of Nathaniel or Nathan Field, whose name is seventeenth in the Folio list, indicates the way in which careers developed. Born in 1587 he was the son of a preacher who denounced the stage and sent him to St Paul's Grammar School whence Giles lured or snatched him to be one of the Children of the Chapel. His father may have died before he was shocked by the news that his son was engaged in 'Satan's workshop'. Ben Jonson noted his ability, liked him and saw to his further education by teaching him Latin. He was one of the children in two of Jonson's comedies and later appeared in *Epicene* when he was twenty-two. In 1614 he received a striking tribute from Jonson in *Bartholomew Fair* where he is mentioned with Burbage as one of the best actors of the day. He then joined the King's Men but did not stay long.

He became involved in a sexual scandal and this was at a high social level. The Earl of Argyll was reported in 1619 to be paying for the nursing of a child 'which the world says is daughter to my Lady and N. Field the player'. The versatile Nathan collaborated in play-writing with the leading dramatists of the day including Fletcher and Massinger. The whispering world may have slandered him as an adulterer, but his portrait at Dulwich shows him to be a handsome fellow who might well have been a captivating lady's man. He is shown as dark-eyed with a medium-sized moustache and unbearded except for a slight tuft below the lower lip. He married and had a family, but died at forty-six. To start life with the Children of the Chapel could have rewarding results. The general accusations made by the implacable enemies of the theatre are not borne out by documented tales of demoralised lives. Halliwell says that Field was 'a notoriously loose liver', but does not supply the evidence. If he did no worse than have a secret amour with a Countess he would not then be thought a desperate sinner and still less might be thought so today.

Was Shakespeare a boy actor in Lancashire, calling himself Shakeshafte, a variant on his family name which had been used by his grandfather? If so he had to hurry back to become Anne Hathaway's lover in Warwickshire. But Shakeshafte was also known as a family name in Shropshire. It is a very thin story and would hardly have been considered had not there been such a consuming interest in the hidden years of Shakespeare's life. The reason for introducing it is that the careful Sir Edmund Chambers thought it worth a chapter called William Shakeshafte in his volume of *Shakespearian Gleanings*. No judgment was passed by him on the validity of the theory.

This supposition was based upon an item in a will made in 1581 by a Lancashire man of property, Alexander Houghton, who left to his brother Thomas 'all my Instrumentes belonging to mewsickes and all manner of playe clothes if he be minded to keppe and do keepe players'. If Thomas was not inclined to accept and maintain actors the legacy passed to Sir Thomas Hesketh of Rufford who was 'most hertelie' required to be friendly to 'ffoke Gyllome and William Shakeshafte', now dwelling with the testator, and to take them into his service or help them to some good master.

Both Houghton and Hesketh visited the Earl of Derby, taking their players with them. The Earl kept a Company; so did his son, Ferdinando, Lord Strange, whose team, known as Derby's or Strange's Men, worked in London in 1591; they co-operated with Henslowe and the Admiral's Men and in 1593 they included Heminge, Pope, Kempe, and Phillips who broke away shortly afterwards to form the Chamberlain's Men. Shakespeare is not mentioned, but Strange's Men had acted *Henry VI, Part I*, which suggests a possible connection. How, when, and why he made the supposed journey to the North is not explained. Shakespeare showed no intimate acquaintance with Lancashire and his plays as he did with his neighbouring Cotswold country and its vocabulary. If he did have some young experience of acting it is far more likely to have been with the Earl of Berkeley's Men. The belief that he was a school-master in the country might refer to a post as tutor at Berkeley Castle which is mentioned in *Richard II* (II, iii). The episode is set in the wilds of Gloucestershire. When Harry Percy is asked, 'How far to Berkeley?' he answers, 'There stands the castle with its tuft of trees.' Why this local and arboreal detail, so strangely familiar to a Northumbrian, if Shakespeare had not a personal memory of the house and its grounds? If he is to be associated as a teenager with a theatrical troupe Gloucestershire is a better candidate than Lancashire for that surmise.

There is natural curiosity about the boys who played the big roles in Shakespeare's plays, but it cannot be satisfied. The Folio list does not help us by identifying players and parts. No other evidence has been found. In 1927 Professor T. W. Baldwin published *The Organisation and Personnel of the Shakespeare Company*. In it he bravely constructed complete cast-lists for all Shakespeare's plays working on the cast-lists of seven plays written by other men and acted by Shakespeare's company. Mr Richard David in his essay on *Shakespeare and the Players*, published along with selected British Academy lectures at the quatercentenary in 1964, had to point out that: 'Unfortunately not one of these surviving lists falls within the period of Shakespeare's working life.' All books about Shakespeare's life have to include conjecture. There is no crime in reasonable surmise. Baldwin carried the guessing game much further than most.

It is most unlikely that any boy had the privilege of being Shakespeare's private pupil. We know something of his London habitations as a lodger. For a time, round about 1604, he was 'rooming' at Silver Street in the Cripplegate ward in the home of Christopher Mountjoy, a maker of costly jewelled tires which adorned the heads of fashionable ladies. There is no evidence that he brought his wife and family to London and set up a household of his own. Leading a single life he was not eligible to take in and train apprentices. The boys went into the care of the married Sharers and lived with their families. Shakespeare's instruction had to be given in the theatre.

It has previously been suggested that he limited his acting in his own plays to small parts in order to supervise rehearsals in which the drilling of the youngest was the hardest work. While the names of his young players and their parts remain unknown some general deductions have been plausibly made about the juvenile casting in the great comedies of 1598 to 1600. There must have been a pair of gifted boys who could be relied upon to memorise long parts, provide a spirited performance, and give the requisite sparkle to the banter and riposte of the quick-witted women. One of them, the taller, played Beatrice, Rosalind, and Viola, perhaps two Rosalinds since there was a revival of *Love's Labour's Lost* in a 'corrected and augmented version' in 1598. The smaller took Hero, Celia, and Maria. The difference in physical size is indicated in the text. That partnership may have begun with Portia and Nerissa. It had ended by the time of the great tragedies. Ophelia and Desdemona, both of whom had to have singing voices, and Cordelia need a different type of player.

Simplicity in suffering was essential. The young masters of the witty line had had their day.

The quips of the boy players were conversational and showed their smartness in delivering the neat verbal exchanges of 'a pleasant conceited comedy', as so many entertainments were then called. On the public stages they cannot have been looking for laughs by what is now called camping or drag in theatrical slang. This is sometimes neatly satirical and sometimes buffoonery. Since it was generally accepted that women's parts would have masculine casting and there was no expectation of seeing an actress on the stage until Mrs Hughes appeared as Desdemona in the reopening of the theatres in 1660, there would have been no fun and probably some disgust if the youth playing a wanton had overdone the oeillades and added camping to the seductive methods.

That could happen at a private party. Mr Baker is justified in citing as an example of drag the antics of Dicky Robinson at 'a gossip's feast' where he appeared as a lawyer's wife and 'sent frolics'. Actors may have continued to act and men to masquerade as women when their work was done and hospitality was being noisily enjoyed over the drinks, but there is only this one account of such larking. Jonson's mention of Robinson was made eleven years after Shakespeare's death: then King James had been thirteen years on the throne. The morals of his Court would have affected public standards of the permissible joke and the taste of his time was very different from that of Queen Elizabeth.

That the boys' performances of important girls' and women's parts were little noticed in Shakespeare's time is indicated by the sentences added to the title of a play in the Quarto Editions. These naturally advertised the principal causes of the success which led to the printing of the texts, piratical or authorised. The feminine roles are never stressed. In the case of *King Lear* it is mentioned that he had three daughters, but there is particular reference to 'the unfortunate life of Edgar' and his 'sullen and assumed humour of Tom of Bedlam'. The actor of his role had obviously made a hit. There is no mention by name of Edmund, the Fool, or any of the women.

In the case of the Histories the Quartos of course mention as a particular triumph the humours of Falstaff. Pistol must have been a conspicuous success since his is one of the attractions mentioned in the Quarto of *The Merry Wives of Windsor* as well as in that of *Henry IV, Part II*. In the Windsor play attention is drawn to four other men beside Falstaff and Pistol. They are Sir Hugh, Justice Shallow, Master Slender, and Nym. These are small parts compared with that of Ford about whom there is silence. There is no mention of either of the Wives. But soon the Wives were regarded rightly as principal roles.

Apparently they did not count for much when the play was published in 1602. The contributions of some minor men were thought more likely than the boys or youths in skirts to assist sales among those who had seen or heard of the play and might pay sixpence to read it. The centre of interest in *Twelfth Night*, of which there is no Quarto, was Malvolio. That is shown by the fact that Sir Henry Herbert, who become Master of the Revels in 1623, entered in his Office Book of that year 'At Candlemas Malvolio was acted at Court by the King's Servants'. He had forgotten the play's title or else it had been altered by the King's Men for business reasons. They did not think of changing it to Viola. Derisive laughter came before lyric love.

It is misleading to think of the Elizabethan theatre in terms of our own stages and studios where big names are won by sedulous promotion and advertisement. Proficiency there may be; publicity there must be. The newspapers are steadily fed with paragraphs about budding genius and triumphs to be expected. After a successful opening with a newcomer contributing to the hit there is a routine announcement that he or she became 'a star in a night'. This can sometimes be unkind since those who are sent up like rockets may come down with the stick while another blaze is being contrived by the experts in play-house pyrotechnics. The theatre is fortunately less corrupted by nonsensical boosting than the crazy world of the Pop Singers, but in what J. B. Priestley has so well described as the Admass Society advertising must go on if the admiration of a play, a film, or a personality is to be massive.

The player of Juliet may have done even better than Shakespeare expected, but we know nothing of him. His name was not blazoned to an impressionable public. A showman of today, exploiting the clamour about glamour in the mass media, would think that to be a deplorable waste of opportunity. But the boys had no idea of sudden fame and probably accepted their position without rancour. A sensible apprentice to Shakespeare's company knew that he was getting the best possible start. If he kept his head when he lost the treble voice he could expect to move up and mature as a senior player and draw the profits of a Sharer. He might even, like Alleyn and Burbage, at last become the talk of the town.

CHAPTER IX
Danger and Discipline

❧❧

BOTH AS actor and dramatist Shakespeare worked in a dangerous trade. The life was not as hazardous as that of the politician or ambitious courtier over whose shoulder rose the Tower of London and the shadow of the executioner. The player did not risk his neck, but the gaolers of the Fleet and the Marshalsea were round the corner. In the supposedly 'spacious times of great Elizabeth' as Tennyson called them, there was a limited accommodation for freedom of speech. The tongue, as an unruly member, had to be under government on the Bankside as well as in Whitehall.

In one way an actor was safer than the ordinary citizen with a settled occupation. He was mobile. When the plague infested London he could move out, pack his costumes and 'props' and try his luck on tour. That provided a hard, poor life but it was an escape from the knolling of the funeral bell which was the constant music of a city struck by pestilence. But there were risks on the road where the highwaymen did not lurk only for the wealthy traveller.

An anonymous tract printed in May, 1605, recounted the *Pretty Prancke passed by Ratsey on certaine players that he met by chance in an Inne.* Ratsey's dupes thought they were in luck when this rogue heard their play (the part of *Hamlet* was mentioned), praised their quality, and paid them forty shillings, which was far more than they would have taken in the ordinary way of a country-town performance. He then waylaid them and stripped them of their money. The actors lost their cash and Ratsey his life. With victims not so easily fleeced he had been over-daring elsewhere and had been hanged at Bedford before this account of his exploits was printed.

Even with the villains thus despatched from time to time the roads were never secure. But vagabond players had the protection of their poverty. To plunder them was a waste of time. Ratsey's practical joke brought him no great profit. He had gained little more than a free entertainment which he had the taste to appreciate.

The streets of the capital were trouble-spots in which theatre people were sometimes dangerously tangled in a brawl. It has been plausibly suggested that the triangular scuffle in *Romeo and Juliet*, fatal to Mercutio, is based on a memory of what happened to Christopher Marlowe in Hog Lane in 1589. There near Shoreditch, where actors and writers lived to be near the earliest playhouses, he became involved in a duel with one Bradley, an innkeeper's son. Thomas Watson, a poet, tried to part the swordsmen. Marlowe yielded to his persuasion but Bradley rashly turned on Watson and wounded him. Watson struck back, drove his blade into Bradley's breast, and so killed him. Marlowe and Watson were taken to Newgate where the former was kept for thirteen days and then let out on bail. At the subsequent trial Marlowe was exonerated and Watson, though justifiably pleading self-defence, served five months in prison.

Another duellist and a killer was Ben Jonson who in 1598 had fought and lethally wounded Gabriel Spenser, one of Pembroke's Men. Jonson could prove his literacy and so received the 'benefit of clergy' which saved his life and cost him the pain and disgrace of a branded hand. That 'a little learning is a dangerous thing' was not the case in Elizabethan London. It could save a man from the gallows. Such were the chances and hazards of urban life when tempers were lost by men who brought their swords with them when they walked the streets.

There is no record of Shakespeare as a fighting man. It is is obvious from his plays that he knew the lingo and technique of the duel into which the combatants went with a sword in one hand and a dagger in the other. He was thought to be a dangerous character by William Gardiner, a corrupt Justice who demanded security from the alleged menaces of Shakespeare and others in 1596. Gardiner was exposed as a swindler and to be at odds with such a rogue was more a sign of probity than of violent intentions. Shakespeare's company were once in trouble for a stupid indiscretion, of which more will be said, but there is no evidence that they were rash or riotous in their lives. The clash of steel they kept for their plays in which the mimic blood flowed in streams. If Burbage was as ready with a weapon off the stage as he had to be on it only a fool would pick a quarrel with him.

A dagger in a tavern brawl at Deptford ended Marlowe's short fiery life. It also removed him from serious trouble caused by the 'damnable opinions' with which he was charged. He was a free thinker, a free speaker, and jested about the religion which he rejected. In the last weeks of his life the Privy Council was inquiring into accusations of atheism and blasphemy and, if the verdict had gone against him, the penalty would have been extremely severe. Shakespeare was not one of the Raleigh set who talked audaciously on controversial or unusual topics. He was not by education or inclination a speculative thinker about the universe. He took the orthodox view of the cosmic order while he observed the ways of men on earth and reflected humanely on humanity. He knew his place as a member of an acting company favoured by a Queen and a King and carrying the name of their Chamberlains. Orthodoxy there had to be. If he doubted, it was not in public.

None the less there is a puzzle about the presentation of political opinion in his plays. In *Troilus and Cressida* (I, iii) Ulysses delivers a long speech about law and order which has little relevance to the Greek army camped outside beleaguered Troy. The railing of Thersites against the generals is made the excuse for it, but the vituperations of that foul-mouthed scold hardly called for a major exposition of political theory and a comprehensive statement of conservative views about the constitution and regulation of society. The stars over man's head stay or move in order; they 'observe degree, priority, and place'. So, it is argued, the men below must be instructed by the heavens above to respect rank and authority. At the summit of 'degree' was the monarch. Below him or her, social grading from lords to commons was for Ulysses (and Shakespeare) the foundation of civil peace.

> *O, when degree is shaked,*
> *Which is the ladder to all high designs,*
> *The enterprise is sick! How could communities,*
> *Degrees in schools, and brotherhoods in cities,*
> *Peaceful commerce from dividable shores,*
> *The primogenity and due of birth,*
> *Prerogative of age, crowns, sceptres, laurels,*
> *But by degree, stand in authentic place?*
> *Take but degree away, untune that string,*
> *And, hark, what discord follows!*

The case for conformity in a State where rank was respected in its many tiers could not have been more amply and eloquently put forward.

Yet in the plays we find kings, noblemen, and prelates presented without mitigation as marauders, murderers, and slaves of vile ambition. As Bernard Shaw said of these characters, 'Surely a more mercilessly exposed string of scoundrels never crossed the stage.' He wondered, 'What was the real nature of the mysterious restraint which kept "Eliza and James" from teaching Shakespeare to be civil to crowned heads?' The answer must be that what went on in the past was far away and long ago. Being rulers in their own day, they saw themselves as very different people from the previous occupants of their thrones. Queen Elizabeth could claim that she was one of the Tudors who had brought to her country peace and prosperity at home, victory at sea, and a high European renown for advance in the arts and graces. The ravaged, fratricidal England of the Wars of the Roses could be presented in the mimicry of play-acting; it was good, gory stuff for a public which, including herself, delighted in the bloody spectacles of the Bear Garden. To show the ancient history of Scotland as a shambles need not disgust King James since it was carefully established by the dramatist that Banquo, from whom James claimed descent, was a victim of royal villainy and not its contriver.

It is worth noting that when Shakespeare (or Shakespeare and Fletcher) came to recent history in *Henry VIII* the play ended with a most humble and eloquent salute to the dead Queen and her successor. Elizabeth was not there to hear the speech of Cranmer written for her christening, but if she had been she would have had no cause for teaching Shakespeare to be 'civil to crowned heads'. The babe's future life is to be 'a pattern to all princes living', wise, virtuous, and exemplary, while

> *Those about her*
> *From her shall read the perfect ways of honour.*

There follows a scarcely justified but doubtless most acceptable tribute to King James who

> *Shall star-like rise as great in fame as she was*

and then so shine that

> *our children's children*
> *Shall see this and bless heaven.*

King Henry, in reply to Cranmer's fulsome forecast of the glories to accompany Elizabeth's reign, says:

> *The oracle of comfort has so pleased me*
> *That, when I am in heaven, I shall desire*
> *To see what this child does.*

The King's confidence about his celestial future may have raised an irreverent smile in some of the audience while both monarchs had been given a welcome to suit the utmost demands of their vanity by a dramatist who was very far from needing lessons in prudence and politeness.

To Shakespeare's public there was no shaking of degree and no slandering of royalty when the criminal Kings of the past were strutting their hour on the stage. They had gone long ago and had been happily and gloriously replaced.

If offence were given by an unpleasant incident or regrettable line it could go 'to the barber's'. An example of such cutting occurred in the reference in *Hamlet* to the sottishness of the heavy-drinking Danes. This had vanished when the Editors of the First Folio printed a text slightly shorter than that of the Second Quarto. Shakespeare may have been repeating some comments on the habits of Elsinore brought home by Kempe, Pope, and Bryan who had toured in Denmark in 1586 long before they joined the Chamberlain's Men. Such gossip had to go. When Princess Anne of Denmark became the Queen of England caution was called for.

Shakespeare worked in a competitive and commercial theatre where money had to be made if life was to go on. In London, and especially on tour, there was the danger of financial disaster. Royal and lordly protection might bring an occasional gift from a patron, but there is no sign of regular subsidy on which the hard-pressed players could rely. The noblemen were great spenders on personal luxury and foppery. If they were eager to cut a dash they did not cut their costs; they would sell an estate to suit their vanity or cope with the result. A sudden appeal to a milord for a grant-in-aid made by a harassed company carrying his name would be low on his gratuity list if there were other and powerful creditors pressing. The team protected by the second Earl of Pembroke was not rescued by its patron when its members had been driven out of town in the plague year of 1593 and were having a rough time on tour. Henslowe recorded that they could not 'save their charges with travel' (i.e. pay their way) 'on the road' and were forced to pawn their costumes to keep alive. Shakespeare had done some work for Pembroke's troupe before he fortunately was taken into the comparative security of the Lord Chamberlain's Men. Since they were a part of the royal establishment and 'on the strength', as we say now, a primary concern was not to be pushed off it. Players had to play safe.

If they moved into the country they could save their lives, but they lost the most rewarding part of their work. Packing up and jogging on from one small audience to another was hard labour and there are records of the King's Men's scanty takings. At Marlborough, a convenient stopping place on the road to

Bath, 'the house' was worth only six shillings. In London audiences were fickle. There could be miserably poor attendance. Leonard Digges, whose verses in praise of Shakespeare were included in the Second Folio of 1640, described the reception of Shakespeare's most popular characters, Othello, Falstaff, Beatrice, Benedick and Malvolio at whose appearance

> *You scarce shall have room,*
> *All is so pestered.*

This he contrasted with the absenteeism of the public at Ben Jonson's plays, even his best such as *Volpone* and *The Alchemist* whose receipts

> *have scarce defrayed the Sea-coale fire*
> *And door-keepers.*

(So the half-open theatres may have been partly heated in winter, but where were those fires, potentially dangerous, placed and how much heat could they distribute? Perhaps Digges had only a roofed play-house in mind.) Jonson, who would have been glad to see a play-house 'pestered' for one of his pieces, had cause for jealousy, but he swallowed his chagrin and could hardly have written more handsomely of his rival in his tributary verses for the First Folio. In addition to the capricious taste of the public there was in the half-open theatres such as the Globe the danger of ruinous weather. Webster attributed the small audience of *The White Devil* in 1612 to production in 'so dull a time of winter and in so open and black a theatre'. The climate had its place in the hazards of a player's life.

Having somehow recovered from their disaster on tour Pembroke's Men, who had been saved by the pawnbroker, got to work again. One of their productions was Nashe's play *The Isle of Dogs*, which was seen and suppressed in 1597. The text has been lost and so the offence which it gave is unknown. It led to prosecution on a charge of containing 'very seditious and slanderous matter'. Ben Jonson was doubly involved as player and collaborator in the writing. From the end of July until the beginning of October he was in the Marshalsea Prison along with his fellow-actors Spenser and Shaw. It was not a long sentence but meant a stop in whatever meagre pay they were getting. There was physical hardship too. Elizabethan gentlemen of title were well accommodated when for various reasons they 'went down' or, in the case of the Tower, up to incarceration. Southampton, though he had been guilty of treason and had only just escaped with his head on his shoulders, had two rooms and visitors, his books, and his cat for company in the Tower and, when ill, was attended by an eminent doctor. A player did not purge his offence so comfortably. But he could go on the run. Dekker, the man most responsible for the folly of *The Isle of Dogs* since he was the principal author, outran the constables and escaped to Yarmouth.

Shakespeare had some early and successful collaboration with this unfortunate troupe. The third part of *Henry VI* was 'sundry times acted by them'. The first Quarto of his very popular *Titus Andronicus* records its performance by three companies who carried the names and protection of three Earls, Derby, Pembroke, and Sussex. When he joined the Chamberlain's Men as a Sharer in 1594 he was on much more solid ground and prudently stayed there.

They had one risky episode in their otherwise steady progress without offence given or taken. On this single occasion the Chamberlain's Men had to face an official inquiry into their choice of a play. That was early in February, 1601, when the Earl of Essex, with Southampton and other malcontents at Whitehall, determined to 'surprise the Court and the Queen's person'. That done she would be ordered to dismiss the enemies of this 'knot', a word used by Shakespeare for the conspirators in *Julius Caesar*, accept King James VI of Scotland as the successor after her death to the English throne, summon Parliament and 'alter the government'.

This was not a direct threat of deposition as a necessary consequence of the insurrection, but it was plainly a treasonable rebellion which could not possibly be tolerated for a moment by the imperious Gloriana. She was at once aware of what was curiously described as 'a general charme and muttering'. An early meaning of 'charm', according to the *Oxford English Dictionary*, is 'a blended noise, as of birds or school-children', and the Essex faction showed an almost infantile silliness in thinking that London would support their insurrection. A few muttered in the streets. Far more people regarded the rebels with resentment and disdain. The reckless push for power was a fatal fiasco and, with the exception of the fortunate Southampton, the leaders of the 'knot' were beheaded after trial in the following month.

The Chamberlain's Men had been silly too. Their hazardous involvement was caused by an invitation to play Shakespeare's *Richard II* as a substitute for one of the *Henry IV* plays at the Globe Theatre. The plotters had dined at midday on the Saturday before the revolt 'at Gunter's' near the Temple and, perhaps hilarious, crossed by water to the South Bank and thought of a device to show that crowned heads could fall. Why not revive *Richard II*? One of the scheming play-goers was Sir Gilly Meyricke, steward to Essex and described by Dr Rowse as 'the Welsh swordsman'. Under examination after the failure of the plot he said that he 'could not tell who procured the play, but thought it was Sir Charles Percye'. Meyricke saw the performance and testified that it included 'the killing of Kyng Richard the second played by the Lord Chamberlens players'.

For some reason unknown Heminge, who usually spoke for the company, was not called when they were 'examined'. It was represented by Augustine Phillips, a senior and trusted member who in this case was acting as treasurer. He explained that a day or two before a group of titled men

'spak to some of the players in the presans of thys examinate to have the play of the deposyng and killing of Kyng Richard the second to be played the next Saterday, promising to get them forty shillings more than their ordynary.' (State Papers)

The actors, probably too busy with their own affairs to realise what mischief was afoot, made an objection to the proposal and did it for the wrong reason. They argued that this would be unprofitable because the play was 'so old and so long out of use'. Evidently the offer of extra money, added to their own surprising ignorance of danger in the air, won them over. So, according to the report of the State Trial of Sir Gilly, Phillips accepted the two pounds 'besides whatsoever he could get'.

The play did not acclaim the deposition and the murder. Far from it. But the crimes were there to be seen and might be a stimulant. In our time there is frequent argument about the effects of the violence and killings to be seen in films and television, although the good men always out-shoot or get the better of the villains. Lytton Strachey in his *Elizabeth and Essex* commented that Sir Gilly must have been 'more conversant with history than literature'; for how otherwise could he have imagined that 'the spectacle of the pathetic ruin of Shakespeare's minor poet of a hero could have nerved any man on earth to lift a hand against so oddly different a ruler'. The examiners evidently decided that the players had been pawns in a game which they did not understand. No penalty was recorded. They were soon back in the Queen's approval, since they gave a command performance on Shrove Tuesday, February 24. Essex was beheaded on the following day. The examination of Phillips had taken place on February 18. It was a speedy return to grace and favour. There is no mention of Shakespeare being involved as a member of the company. Nor in the various examinations was he named as the author.

But there is a curious sequel. The Queen forgave the players, but she did not forget the choice of the play. Indeed it seems to have lingered in her memory in a haunting way. This information came from the papers of the Lambard family, one of whom was an antiquary appointed to be Keeper of the Records in the Tower of London. On August 4, 1601, he visited the Queen in her Privy Chamber at Greenwich. There

He presented her Majestie with his Pandecta of all her rolls, bundells, membranes, and parcells that be reposed in her Majestie's

Tower at London; whereof she had given to him the charge 21st
January last past. . . . She proceeded to further pages, and asked
where she found cause of stay. . . . He expounded these all
according to their original diversities . . . so her Majestie fell upon
the reign of King Richard II saying, 'I am Richard II. Know ye
not that?'

W.L. 'Such a wicked imagination was determined and attempted
   by a most unkind Gent. the most adorned creature that ever
   your Majestie made.'

Her Majestie. 'He that will forget God, will also forget his bene-
   factors; this tragedy was played fortie times in open streets and
   houses.'

This statement about numerous performances is not elsewhere
confirmed. It was not urged against Meyricke and his associates
that they had organised a tour of the town or that the Chamberlain's Men had undertaken it. It is possible that the Queen was
becoming confused. The conversation with Lambard took place
six months after the severe shock of the Essex rebellion and the
execution of the antagonist whom she had once greatly admired.
It had been a shattering experience for an old and anguished
woman. She was approaching the end which came in March, 1603.
Some mental disturbance, in which the revival of *Richard II* took
a distorted prominence, seems likely. She was still seeing herself
as a possible victim of deposition.

   However that may be she could hardly have made the remarks
reported by Lambard unless it were the habit of the players, even
those of her own Household, to visit 'open streets and houses'.
That they were invited to perform in the mansions of the noblemen we know. But the idea of frequent performance in the streets
is surprising. The Queen may have been referring to inn-yards
and the adjective 'open' may indicate that spaces rather than
streets were used. The London roads were narrow and notoriously
crowded and noisy. We learn from *Hamlet* that the actors were
ready to answer any summons, expected to perform in any kind
of chamber and even to lace their text with new speeches

suddenly composed for the occasion. But it is indeed surprising to hear of the Queen's belief that her own company, regularly seen in her palaces, in public theatres and sometimes in private houses, also found time for frequent appearances with plays or episodes from their plays in the middle of the town. If Lambard accurately reported the Queen's allusion to acting round the streets we must alter our ideas of the life led by Shakespeare and his colleagues.

The performances in these conditions must have been rough and scrappy, but sufficiently rewarding to make them worth while. How was money collected from the standers-by and lookers-on? Was the hat passed as by street musicians? Notions of the dignity and quality of the Elizabethan theatre must be revised if this was a common practice. With a mob-audience possibility of giving offence to authority was increased. There was more need than ever for the caution which was not shown when Sir Gilly Meyricke and his friends got the players into trouble for the consideration of two pounds.

The supply, quality, and propriety of entertainment at the Palaces were part of the onerous duties of the Lord Chamberlain. His other cares included the proper maintenance of the royal apartments and wardrobe and the entertainment of guests. Since he worked for testy and choleric sovereigns his office was no sinecure. That the great occasions of State were under his survey is shown by Shakespeare's inclusion of two characters holding this post in the play of *Henry VIII*. At Wolsey's banquet and revel (I, iv) the first of the Chamberlains looks after the tactful seating of the guests.

> *Sweet ladies will it please you sit? Sir Henry,*
> *Place you that side; I'll take charge of this.*
> *His Grace is entering: nay, you must not freeze;*
> *Two women placed together makes cold weather.*

At the end of the play (V, iii) when the christening of Queen Elizabeth is to take place his successor, Lord Sands, orders the porters to keep back the crowds in the Palace-Yard, curses them

as 'lazy knaves' who seem to be letting in their 'faithful friends o'
the suburbs' and cries:

> *Go, break among the press and find a way out*
> *To let the troops pass fairly, or I'll find*
> *A Marshalsea shall hold you for two months.*

Shakespeare knew the palace procedure and its problems from
close acquaintance. As an Actor Sharer in one of the companies
under the Chamberlain's supervision he was sworn in as a 'Groom
of the Chamber in ordinary without fee' and received winter and
summer liveries; at the Coronation of King James in March,
1604, he was at the head of the nine players who were given
four-and-a-half yards of scarlet cloth for their equipment. He
knew the ways of pomp and ceremony by personal experience
and the discipline to be observed.

The much occupied Chamberlain delegated the selection of
players companies and vigilance over their conduct to the Master
of the Revels and his staff. His office had been created by that
revelling King, Henry VIII, and his original function was to
organise an abundance of royal entertainment. Later he became
the watch-dog of the antics and exercised a veto with punitive
measures for disobedience.

During most of Shakespeare's life in the theatre the actors'
overlord, serving under the Lord Chamberlain as Master of the
Revels, was Edward Tilney who held the office from 1579 to
1610. He acquired prohibitive as well as permissive powers
extending far beyond the palaces and was appointed to 'order and
reform, authorise, and put down' all plays offered for public
performance. Thus he became a Censor of texts since it would be
useless to intervene after the public performance of work deemed
'seditious and scurrilous'. The mob would then have had the
poison injected. In 1607 his rule was extended to the publishers
of plays. He then became deputy to the Archbishop of Canterbury
who with his advisers granted licences for all printed books.
The regulations were strict since 'An Act to Restraine Abuses of
Players' had been passed in 1606. Thenceforward 'in any Stage

Play, Interlude, Shewe, Maygame or Pageant those jestingly or profanely speaking or using the holy Name of God or of Christ Jesus or of the Holy Ghost or the Trinity' were liable to a fine of ten pounds for every such offence.

This ruling was applied to Shakespeare's texts. Oaths and words under veto which had been printed in the early Quartos were removed from later editions and from the Folio. The Book-Keeper had also to watch his prompt copy and keep it cleansed of any old offence or newly inserted gag. Ten pounds was large money and there had to be no slips which could mulct the players of as much as their total fee for a Command Performance. F. E. Halliday in his excellent notes on the Censorship in his *Shakespeare Companion* points out how far the vigilance was carried. It was evidently dangerous to mention the devil though why Satan should share the protection given to God is hard to understand. Students of slang who wonder why 'What the dickens' found its way into the text of *The Merry Wives of Windsor* are reminded that in the Quarto of 1602 the words were 'What the devil'. That had to go. Nowhere else does dickens appear in the Folio.

Until the Censorship of Plays was abolished in 1968 British dramatists complained bitterly about the deletion from their scripts of language deemed offensive by the Lord Chamberlain's advisers. (That some of it was remarkably filthy by normal standards was explained to me during an interview with a senior member of his staff who showed me a specimen of the dialogue provided by an ardent exponent of 'social realism'. It was astonishing stuff.) Since the Censorship of plays, as recently practised in Great Britain, did not begin until 1734, some of the most voluble and less informed may have thought that in the theatre of Shakespeare's time there was great freedom of speech. There was not, but the discipline was limited to politics and religion.

All Censorship is bound to have its absurdities since taste in propriety alters quickly and what is a harmless jest to one man is outrageous to another. The Act intended to restrain 'Abuses of Players' did not interfere with quips and puns which seem daring and even disgusting now and not only to those animated by Thomas Bowdler's resolve to save the play-goers and readers from 'Whatever is unfit to be read aloud by a gentleman in the company of ladies'. The greatest ladies of 1600 would not have worried at the frankness so painful to Mr Bowdler. If they talked with the freedom of some of Shakespeare's feminine characters they could hold their own in smutty conversation.

The Master of the Revels was obviously not shocked by the innuendoes of Shakespeare's heroines or the gross jests of his bawds and panders. His business was to safeguard the monarchy and the social order from an insolent or subversive suggestion which could lead to riot or rebellion. He was also a defender of the Christian faith and its Trinity. He was not dictating to the public the limits of its secular laughter as long as the mirth and mockery did not include the dignity and security of Church and State.

While God was thus officially protected, Mammon was not forgotten. The Master of the Revels charged fees for the licences which he granted to the Actor Sharers and House Sharers of theatrical companies, enabling them to set up in the capital or go on tour. The Jacobean King's Men had to give him the proceeds of two benefit performances annually. In theory play-acting was forbidden during Lent, but in fact dispensation was frequently given—for a fee. That was another of Tilney's perquisites. A major scandal of the age was the granting of monopolies in trade, a privilege of the Crown and a profit to the noblemen who secured them. The Master of the Revels, whose official salary was only ten pounds a year, had a share in this racket, a minor share compared with the monopolies in wine, but plainly worth the getting and selling.

When Sir Henry Herbert became Master in 1623 he bought the job from his predecessor for an annual consideration of one hundred and fifty pounds. Herbert's Office Book has not survived, but early Shakespearian scholars had it for use. It reveals the frequency and extent of this traffic. Heminge was constantly coming to him with money in hand. A 'Lent allowance' in 1626 cost the King's Men two pounds. A benefit presentation of

Othello three years later was worth nine pounds and sixteen shillings to the Master. In the same year he received from Heminge for 'a courtesy done him about the Blackfriars house' three pounds. It was one of Bernard Shaw's understandable grievances that he had to pay the Lord Chamberlain two guineas for reading a play which he could and sometimes did reject altogether. That was common practice in the régime of Herbert who refused a play of Massinger's because it contained 'dangerous matter, as the deposing of Sebastian King of Portugal'. The Master of the Revels throve on tips but he dared not take a bribe to pass dangerous matter. He added in his record that in Massinger's case the rejection did not excuse payment. He had his fee notwithstanding, 'which belongs to me for reading it over and ought always to be brought always with the book'. The repetition of 'always' reveals a keen eye for the money. There had to be cash on delivery of a script and no whining for credit until a play had been passed and was paying its way.

A play which had been read and passed was not necessarily safe, as the Chamberlain's Men discovered in the case of *Richard II*. We do not know the arguments which Augustine Phillips used on their behalf: he would surely have said that the play had been licensed originally and that plea apparently prevailed. But there were companies who rashly took a chance with work not submitted to Tilney. If *The Isle of Dogs* was fairly accused of containing 'very seditious and slanderous matter' he was very careless in failing to notice it, demanding an emended script, and saving the players from prosecution. If the players were in urgent need of something to offer quickly—and in the theatrical conditions of the time with no 'long runs' possible that was always likely to happen—they were extremely foolish to rush the piece on without permit and incur the very damaging penalty of imprisonment.

That Tilney kept a sharp eye for dangerous topics is shown by his insistence on alterations in the script of a play on *Sir Thomas More*, whose rewritten manuscript survives. Its original authorship and date of composition are unknown, but the case for Shakespeare's participation in the revision has been strongly argued on grounds of handwriting, spelling, style and compassionate opinion. This occurs in a passage of one hundred and forty-seven lines in which More appears as an advocate of tolerance and appeasement when immigrants are threatened with violence. Shakespeare's share with several others, plausibly identified as Heywood, Chettle, and Munday, is only likely if the play were written and the dispute arose before he had joined the Chamberlain's Men in constant employment as actor and author with a share in the management and profits. Why should he then do an odd job to oblige their rivals? Before that he could, as a free-lance, have accepted a small task of this kind if he wanted to make a little extra money.

The matter is important because, if the passage is in Shakespeare's hand, it is the only sizeable example of his script. But it does not affect the present subject, the condition of the actors and the discipline imposed on their productions. *Sir Thomas More* provides evidence of Tilney's vigilance and of the methods used when he intervened. Orders given were orders taken. There is no news of further trouble. Both the Master of the Revels by his ruling and the dramatists by their obedience were doing their job. There was then no campaigning against the tyranny of the Censorship. The players and playwrights knew where that would land them. Always detested by some they lived by sufferance and had to earn it.

In his steeply graded society the Lord Chamberlain belonged to the higher ranks of the nobility; usually he was an Earl, sometimes a Lord. The Master of the Revels never rose beyond knighthood and did not always win that recognition. It is curious that Tilney, although he held his post for thirty-one years and greatly enlarged its dominion over the players, did not become Sir Edward. There is nothing known of his financial methods. Our information about the perquisites comes from Sir Henry Herbert whose career in the Revels Office began in 1623 when he was twenty-eight and lasted for fifty years, including a long break during the Puritan ascendancy.

The Lord Chamberlain, as one of three senior members of the

Royal Household, was usually a wealthy man with his dignity to maintain; he would hardly peddle licences to perform for small sums. One of King James's Chamberlains, Robert Carr, who was made Earl of Somerset, was notoriously ambitious and unscrupulous. He had larger ideas of filling his pocket than by this kind of petty traffic. His rule over the players, 1613–14, was short. His successors were the Herbert brothers, the Earls of Pembroke and Montgomery.

Fortunately for the theatre the Chamberlains were often theatre-lovers and themselves patrons of companies. One of these, Lord Howard of Effingham, the Lord High Admiral whose fleet destroyed the Spanish Armada, gave his title to the Admiral's Men whose star was Edward Alleyn. He was followed by Henry Carey, Lord Hunsdon, who had his own team before he became responsible for the Chamberlain's Men led by Burbage, Shakespeare, and Kempe. The actors were not so lucky when, after his death in 1596, William Brooke, Lord Cobham, had a brief taste of power in the theatre. He sided with the Puritans in preventing the opening by James Burbage of a new private theatre in Blackfriars and made trouble for Shakespeare who had taken over the name of Sir John Oldcastle from a play on *The Early Victories of Henry V* for the companion of Prince Hal in his *Henry IV* plays. Since Oldcastle had an important place by marriage in Cobham's family tree, the Chamberlain would not allow his name to be smeared by association with Shakespeare's cowardly rogue. The dramatist under pressure chose Sir John Falstaff because there need be no alteration of the text where Sir John was mentioned. Sir John Fastolfe, a character in *Henry VI, Part I* (III, ii), is also a character with no appetite for danger.

> *Whither away, Sir John Fastolfe, in such haste?*
>
> FASTOLFE: *Whither away! to save myself by flight:*
> *We are like to have the overthrow again.*
>
> CAPTAIN: *What! will you fly, and leave Lord Talbot?*
>
> FASTOLFE: *Ay,*
> *All the Talbots in the world, to save my life.*

If Lord Cobham had been less touchy and more prescient and had left Oldcastle in Shakespeare's texts he would have brought lasting renown to his family. The character who became Falstaff was to prove so monstrously memorable in his frauds and follies that he would have immortalised the name of Oldcastle. Falstaff, however, is certainly the better name for the part and the players and Shakespeare were in luck when they had to substitute the two syllables for the clumsy three. Falstaff created an adjective. Oldcastle could not have done that. Falstaffian wit sounds excellent. Oldcastellan would never have done. Cobham's fussiness really was beneficial to all the actors who have embellied themselves for the role.

There was also an intervention in *The Merry Wives of Windsor* at the point where Ford changes his assumed name to Cobham's family name of Brooke. This was altered to Broome in the First Folio. It is a trifle, but indicates the tetchiness of the one Chamberlain and the awareness of the players that it was well to oblige in small matters and so avoid disturbance in big ones. Lord Cobham was succeeded by the second Lord Hunsdon for the wedding of whose daughter Elizabeth to Lord Berkeley in 1596 some think that *A Midsummer Night's Dream* was written. His own team, Hunsdon's Men, seem to have been merged with the Chamberlain's Men. It would have been unsuitable for the Chamberlain to be the patron of a private company in rivalry with that favoured and protected by the Queen.

When the Chamberlain's Men became the King's Men there were no disputes with authority. Tilney retained his place at the Revels Office and was busier than ever since the new King and his Queen were great lovers of professional acting and of amateur masquerades at Court. Shakespeare's fellowship prospered; their sufferings from vigilance and Censorship had never been severe and, despite their blunder with *Richard II*, none of them is known to have been in prison.

CHAPTER X

The Patrons

❦

PATRONAGE WAS given by the nobility in two forms. The poets and sonneteers dedicated their work to men and women of wealth in gratitude for past favours or in hope of favours to come. The ladies of the great houses were highly educated, could appreciate good writing, and were pleased to receive these salutes which began at the royal summit of a cultured society. Edmund Spenser naturally offered *The Faerie Queene* to Queen Elizabeth and then included a letter to Sir Walter Raleigh expounding 'his whole intention'. He also addressed in Sonnet form ten noblemen, two Countesses and 'all the gratious and beautifull Ladies in the Court'.

Samuel Daniel dedicated his 'Delia' sonnets to the Countess of Pembroke declaring himself 'vowed to your honour in all observancy for ever'. But she was no monopolist of his devotion. He also offered poems to the Countess of Bedford, the Countess of Cumberland and her daughter, Lady Anne Clifford. It is difficult not to be curious about the dividends accruing from such literary investment. Were there direct gifts of money, the purchase of a large number of copies, or only a gracious letter of acknowledgement with an invitation to a party where more friends might be made and influence gained? For some of the poets there was a chance to use the by-products of a teacher's life. For the most fortunate there could be a tutorship with bed and board in the stately home. Daniel had that in the Pembrokes' country mansion, Wilton. There the second Countess, born Mary Sidney and brother to Sir Philip of the Leicester House literary group, mingled the culture of her family with the estates and status of the Herberts. There is no evidence that Shakespeare was repaid for his dedications to the Earl of Southampton by a room with a view over the

Titchfield lawns and a place, not far below the salt, at a well-spread table. But it is a likely explanation of his escape from the plague during the terrible visitation of 1593.

Plays printed in quarto rarely carried a dedication. Shakespeare never offered any of his dramatic work to Southampton after dedicating to him in a dignified way his two epics. This friendship brought to the poet, according to Rowe, a substantial gift of money. How it was used is uncertain, perhaps to establish his family in New Place, known as the Great House of Stratford, perhaps to buy shares in the Chamberlain's Men. If the sum was really as large as a thousand pounds there was plenty for both, since New Place was bought for sixty. I have surmised that Southampton may have encouraged and even commissioned the early version of *Love's Labour's Lost* and it is possible that a performance of the comedy was given to entertain Queen Anne at Southampton House in London in 1605. But there is no existing documentary evidence to show that the Earl, who must have admired *Venus and Adonis* and *Lucrece*, ever had any connection with Shakespeare's work in the theatre. The absence of such news may be an accident. But it is odd that Southampton was not mentioned by Heminge and Condell in their introductions of the First Folio in which two other patrons, the Earls of Pembroke and Montgomery, were acclaimed for the favours shown by them to the playwright and flattered with the adjective 'incomparable'.

Southampton, though deeply and dangerously involved in the Essex conspiracy and rebellion, was not named among the men of title who arranged the risky revival of *Richard II*. It is generally assumed that he was, at least for a time, fond of plays and a friend of some of the players, but there is nothing to show that he ever was a theatrical patron. Certainly there was no team working under his name. After his release from the Tower on the accession of King James he had public responsibilities as Lord Lieutenant of Hampshire and Keeper of the Isle of Wight in addition to his commercial and colonial interests as an active member of the Virginia Company. That nothing was said in the First Folio concerning his beneficence to Shakespeare suggests that later in life he had lost his interest in poets and players. Had he retained that enthusiasm he might have been Lord Chamberlain and excellent in that office when it fell vacant in 1615, but it went to the Earl of Pembroke.

Aristocratic patronage was essential to the actors. By the Act of 1572 they could not work in public except under the name of one who held the rank of baron or higher in the peerage. It was one of the conspicuous merits of the Elizabethan age that so many of its noblemen were ready to take players under their wing. If the owners of the great houses and estates had been devoted only to their horses and hounds in the country and to their display and dissipation in London, if they had taken the legal as well as the Puritan view that actors were idle rogues and riff-raff and better flogged than favoured, Elizabethan drama could not have emerged. The poets, if they were not employed as tutors who wrote their verses in their leisure, had to make what they could by earning the playwright's petty rewards. If there had been no licences to act there would have been no occupation for a professional dramatist. No Patron, no licence. No licence, no play!

Lords and their ladies with a taste for authorship wrote plays of a somewhat academic kind and these sometimes had literary merit. They also had the sense to realise that a play is only a shadow of itself without an audience. So they promoted lively performance for themselves in their mansions and for the public in the new theatres in London. The upkeep of a team was not burdensome to an owner of large property. Favours were granted but the Patron did not serve as an ever-open purse. When the second Earl of Pembroke's Men went bankrupt on tour he did not rescue them with a subsidy.

A company had their lord's livery which provided a suit of clothes. If they did receive more bounty than his uniform, his blessing and the coveted permisson to perform in public, the gift was exceptional. What mattered to the nation and to the evocation of its genius in poetry was the willingness of the aristocrats to make room for the Muses in what might have been only Horseback Hall in the country or a Bear Garden in the city. Had they limited their attention to their stables, their marriages and their money, like the titled and landowning characters described by Anthony Trollope in the philistine Barchester region, there would have been no theatre and no dramatists. At the top of this precious patronage was the Queen who encouraged her noblemen to encourage actors and so made Shakespeare possible. Had they been deaf to music and poetry and sent no players to London or on tour the man of Stratford must have stayed there as a frustrated schoolmaster or lawyer's clerk.

An early and influential pioneer in theatrical patronage was Robert Dudley, Earl of Leicester. He took the eye of the Queen and held the ear of the Queen. He entertained her at Kenilworth in 1566, 1572, and 1575 with feasts of showmanship and demonstrations of what England could do in its rapidly maturing practice of the arts. For some years he had players in his household. Dudley's Men, as they were first known, had been on tour in 1559. From them, soon known as Leicester's Men, came the development of skilled professional acting in London.

In 1572 an Act of Parliament was passed in order to put some control on the very mixed company and very free trade of strolling players, wandering minstrels, bear-wards, acrobats, mountebanks and the raggle-taggle community of 'vagrom' men who lived by their limbs and wits and the entertainment provided. Under the Act actors were licensed to perform only under royal or aristocratic patronage. In 1574 Letters Patent gave the Queen's permisson to James Burbage and other members of Leicester's Men to 'use, exercise and occupy the art and faculty of playing, comedies, tragedies, stage plays ... for the recreation of our loving subjects and our solace and pleasure'. London soon profited by that law which was both restrictive and permissive. It made patronage the players' entrance and the stage-door through which Alleyn, Burbage, Tarlton, Kempe and later Shakespeare could pass without interference or persecution. The Theatre in Shoreditch was opened in 1576 with Leicester's Men as its first occupants.

Fortunately the fashion for theatrical patronage was infectious. To have players on the domestic strength of a great house became as helpful to the status and reputation of its owner as the presence of the servants and grooms. Ability to entertain guests with a play or pageant was as necessary to high degree as was the provision of banquets and hunting. The grandees liked to display taste in the arts as much as their gallantry at tilting or their readiness for active service on sea or land. Players accompanied their lords to the wars. Leicester's Men were with him in Holland in 1586. At home those who sent out a troupe under their name were indispensable to the amenities of town and country.

The university students were allowed to be busy as amateur actors and provided audiences for the professionals such as the Chamberlain's Men, who took *Hamlet* to Oxford and Cambridge, as the First Quarto of that play tells us. Without the patronage which Leicester had exemplified by organising Dudley's Men when he was twenty-seven and by establishing them in London there might have been no *Hamlet* to act. The Queen had her 'solace and pleasure'. So had her subjects. So has posterity.

It was not Shakespeare who called the Earls of Pembroke and Montgomery the 'Incomparable Pair of Brethren'. Heminge and Condell, the editors of the First Folio, selected that exalting epithet. The dedications of the two epic poems to Southampton by Shakespeare himself are not so fulsome. To call an Earl noble was merely to mention a fact. To speak of a 'strong prop for a weak burthen' was a modest and realistic acknowledgement of valuable support. To speak of the patron's 'honourable disposition' was respectful, probably accurate, and very far from grovelling. There is nothing in either of these introductory salutes to match the attribution of an excellence without equal.

The First Folio was offered in 1623 to 'The Most Noble and Incomparable pair of Brethren, William Earl of Pembroke etc, Lord Chamberlain to the King's Most Excellent Majesty, and Philip, Earl of Montgomery etc, Gentleman of his Majesty's Bed-chamber, both Knights of the most noble order of the Garter and our singular good Lords.' There follow thanks for 'the many favours we have received at your hands', and further gratitude to their lordships who 'have prosecuted both the author and his work with so much favour' while he was alive. There is the hope that they will 'use the like indulgence' to the writings now collected and printed 'as they had done unto their parent'. It is stressed that the Incomparable pair had 'liked the several parts when they were acted.'

Thus it is made plain that the two Earls had enjoyed the plays in the theatre and bestowed their favours both on Shakespeare and his fellowship of players. Of what size and nature these favours were is unknown. It is likely that the Incomparables also added money to their admiration of the playwright and players. Pembroke in his later life was renowned for his generosity. He was a Patron who opened his purse. On his list of beneficiaries was Ben Jonson who was given an annual grant of twenty pounds for the purchase of books, and Ben was not a member of the King's Men whose affairs became the responsibility of both brothers, of William when he was appointed Lord Chamberlain in 1615 and of Philip in 1625.

To hold that office could be exacting. King James and his Danish Queen were eager for entertainment and wanted the best. They spent lavishly on Court Masques and were continually demanding Court Performances. During Pembroke's first winter of office the Chamber Account mentions payments to the King's Men for fourteen different plays. The detailed preparations and the censorship of plays proposed were in the hands of the Master of the Revels but, in cases of dispute and complaint, the final decision went to the Lord Chamberlain. It was essential that the King's Men should not give offence by indiscretion or political clumsiness. Furthermore it was the Chamberlain's business to see that there was no lack of quality in the performance. Pembroke had little direct contact with Shakespeare after he had assumed his position since the latter died early in the following year. The favours mentioned must have come earlier in the way of private patronage and made it certain that he had a high opinion of the entertainment given by the King's Men.

The Lord Chamberlain had more than artistic standards to consider. The Earl of Montgomery, who had succeeded to the Earldom of Pembroke on his brother's death without an heir in 1630 and had taken over the Chamberlain's office in 1625, was called in to decide a financial dispute in 1635. Heminge had died and it seems that his son William secretly sold three shares in the Globe and two in the Blackfriars Theatre, the headquarters of the King's Men, to an outsider called John Shank who paid five hundred and six pounds for this investment. Three of the actors petitioned the Lord Chamberlain for the right to buy these holdings.

Here was an early example of the conflict between the business-man who speculates in the arts and the artists who naturally resent the control of their affairs passing out of their hands. Montgomery, now the fourth Earl of Pembroke, seems to have made a compromise in his decision. Shank had to sell back to the players one share in each theatre. If, as is likely, they held some shares themselves this provided the controlling interest which they sought. To have the Lord Chamberlain well-disposed could be valuable in finance as well as in esteem at the Palace. The exaggerated compliment paid to the Incomparables by the editors of the Folio had not been a waste of words. The Pembrokes kept up a much closer connection with the Jacobean theatre than did Southampton and were Patrons over a much longer period.

Like Lord William Herbert Southampton has been regarded by some scholars and historians and, with great confidence, by A. L. Rowse, as the Sonnet Man. But there again there is no certainty. Yet he has had a predominant and disproportionate place in the vast library which might be indexed as Shakespeariana. Three full-scale biographies have appeared, two in fairly close succession in 1965 and 1968. The publishers of the latter pair obviously decided that the reading public would not be attracted to the subject unless the title of the book carried Shakespeare's name first. The recent volume by Dr Rowse, *Shakespeare's Southampton* (1965), and Professor Akrigg's *Shakespeare and Southampton* (1968) are evidence of that prudent policy. In other words, the poet made the patron saleable. Meanwhile Pembroke, whose career was in many ways similar to Southampton's, has received scanty attention. There is, however, an excellent section on the Incomparable Brethren in Sir Tresham Lever's history of *The Herberts of Wilton*.

The contribution of that family to the culture, graces, intellectual speculation and architecture of the nation in Elizabethan and Stuart times has been undervalued and is quite as much worth consideration as the progress of the Wriothesleys who became the Earls of Southampton. Accordingly I am recounting as typical of the period the fortunes and achievements of the Herberts. In their home there was serenity and scholarship beside the turbulence of town-loving youth fretted by a rusticity whose elegance was not exciting. 'Love is too young to know what conscience is', wrote Shakespeare in a sonnet. That ignorance was shared in the hot-blooded adolescence of Lord William who was to be the third Earl. But there was also in his life a striking change of character. The rake and libertine became the responsible patron of the arts in London and of learning at Oxford University. He proved to be a worthy son of a gifted and generous mother.

At Wilton, where the brothers grew up, there was Elizabethan life in its most varied and stimulating richness. There was not only beauty of landscape and building; there was awareness of beauty and delight in the arts. The boys' mother had indeed a prior claim on the adjective later given to them. The epitaph by William Browne has become an anthology piece:

> *Underneath this sable Herse*
> *Lyes the subject of all verse,*
> *Sydneye's Sister, Pembroke's mother.*
> *Death, ere thou hast slaine another*
> *Ffaire & Learn'd & good as she,*
> *Tyme shall throw a Dart at thee.*

Mary Sidney, who married the Second Earl of Pembroke, was one of the highly educated and studious women known as the Tudor Paragons. Sharing their brothers' tutors in the great houses they were, like the Queen herself, as far advanced in classical and modern learning and as multi-lingual as any winner of scholarships at Somerville and Girton in our time. Mary's brother, Philip Sidney, out of favour with the Queen, stayed at Wilton and worked with her on his prose and poetry and their joint translations. Here, as John Aubrey said, was both Paradise and Academe.

Paradise, it must be remembered, is Greek for a park and Wilton had all the usual richness of a wealthy estate as well as the less usual pursuit of knowledge and the arts. Here were gathered Mary Pembroke's favoured poets, savants, and pioneers of scientific research, Samuel Daniel, Nicholas Breton, Thomas Moffat, who wrote a book on silk-worms, and Adrian Gilbert, half-brother to Sir Walter Raleigh, described by Aubrey as 'a great chymist in those dayes'. The sonneteers and the scientists mingled what are now called the Two Cultures at Mary's table.

Her epitaph included tribute to her goodness. She received many poetic dedications from poets who stressed her virtue. Yet Aubrey libelled the great Countess with his nasty rubbish about her character. He alleged that her father-in-law kept her from the Court in London fearing that she would make a cuckold of his son. He also said,

'She was very salacious, and she had a contrivance that in the spring of the yeare when the stallions were to leap the mares they were to be brought before such a part of the house, where she had a *vidette* to look on them and please herself with their sport; and then she would act the like sport herself with *her* stallions. One of her great gallants was crooke-back't Cecill, earl of Salisbury.'

It has been said that 'a dirty mind is a continual feast'. This may be cynicism or realism. Undeniably Aubrey, so enchanting a gossip in many ways, relished any banquet of smutty stories. Wilton was a virtuous and Protestant household. Nicholas Breton wrote of a notable home where were

'God daily served, religion truly preached, all quarrels avoided, peace carefully preserved, swearing not heard of, truth easilie believed, a table fully furnished, a house richly garnished, honour kindly entertained, vertue highly esteemed, service well rewarded, the poor blessedly relieved, and kindnesse was a companion in every corner of the house.'

He did not name the house, but since he had fed at that table and sipped the cultural fountain it is obvious to what Palace of Truth and Piety he refers.

The atmosphere could be rather bleak for growing boys preferring the paradisal gardens, the stables, and the grounds to the school-room and its tutors. The inconsistent Aubrey first maligned the morals of the Countess and then praised the scholastic company which she kept. 'In her time Wilton was like a College, there were so many learned and ingeniose persons. She was a great chymist and spent yearly a great deale in that study.' There were then no professors of juvenile psychology and no thought of the now fashionable 'disturbance and maladjustment' said to be caused by deprivations and repressions. The young Lord William Herbert grew up to be a wild youth and had a taste of prison when he was twenty. Philip never got over an ungovernable temper and a quick, loose tongue. It is unfair to think that the parents and their attendant bevy of 'ingeniose persons' had disinclined their sons to profit by the Academe and increased a natural inclination of boyhood to prefer sport to bookishness and of youth to find silk hose on feminine legs more attractive than blue stockings?

Whether or not the academic atmosphere was oppressive to the maturing boys there was another and worse burden to be borne. This was the matrimonial scheming over the heads of children who might find themselves affianced soon after they were ten. That was the common practice in the great Elizabethan families for whom marriage was chiefly a financial deal. There was lengthy and contentious argument about settlements and dowries. It must seem to us a repulsive as well as absurd

procedure. If the wealthy families or ambitious poor ones of today
do have such bargaining in mind they do not begin to plan while
the boys and girls are still of 'prep school' age.

The daughter of a Cheshire knight, Ann Fitton, younger sister
of the notorious Mall, Pembroke's mistress, went through a
token marriage with John Newdigate of Arbery in Warwickshire
at the age of twelve. Her father knew exactly what were her
husband's settled expectations. Socially and financially it could be
called 'a good match'. This one chanced to be also a happy one.
When the pair came together eight years later they found the
contrived partnership agreeable and it fruitfully endured.

But spirited boys rebelled against this trafficking and asserted
at least some freedom of choice in a matter which so decisively
shaped their future lives. No period has excelled the Elizabethan
in the praise of young love with poetry both delicate and passionate. Yet in the arrangement of a wedding love very often had no
place. The poor were luckier. Shakespeare's marriage may or
may not have been a folly, but certainly neither he nor Anne
Hathaway could have been potential assets for their parents in a
property deal.

The gentry believed that their estates had to be sustained and
enlarged and there was no shame about this chaffering over the
young pawns in the game. The system was bound to create
miserable unions and subsequent infidelities. Yet it was accepted
usage and the Second Earl of Pembroke was soon busily engaged
on fixing a bride for his boy William. One would expect the
women to have resented this procedure and not least William's
mother, widely praised for her wisdom and her kindness. She
may have protested at the efforts to fix William's future. We
cannot tell. She had no daughter whose sale as a child in the
marriage market might have horrified her.

It must be admitted that the scheming did not begin with the
Pembrokes nor did it start when the boy was a mere child. When
he was fifteen Sir George Carey, the heir to Lord Hunsdon who
was then Lord Chamberlain, endeavoured to arrange a marriage
with his daughter. William would have none of that. Two years

later his father had his eye on Lady Bridget Vere, the daughter of the Earl of Oxford and granddaughter of the powerful Lord Burghley. The child was then thirteen. Burghley hesitated, but negotiations continued. Finally it was William who ended the matter by refusing to marry under orders. He went to Court when he was seventeen with no matrimonial strings attached, lived and loved as he chose, had an affair with a Maid of Honour, and was sent in complete disgrace to the Fleet Prison as the putative father of Mall Fitton's child.

By a curious coincidence the other candidate for the honour of having begotten some of the finest Sonnets in the English language, the Earl of Southampton, had a similar experience. He had succeeded to his title when he was eight and became a ward of the State with Lord Burghley as his guardian. Burghley wanted him to marry another of the Earl of Oxford's daughters, Lady Elizabeth Vere. He refused, to the fury of his guardian. Like William Herbert he preferred to anticipate the rites of marriage with a young woman of the Queen's Household at Whitehall, Elizabeth Vernon, a ward and cousin of the Earl of Essex. Also as with Herbert, the affair was embarrassingly fruitful. When Mistress Vernon's pregnancy was discovered the Queen immediately ordered that the guilty partners should be sent to the Fleet Prison. This would have meant extreme suffering for poor people. For persons of high rank such incarceration was not the hardship that befell humbler persons. Miss Vernon had 'the sweetest and best appointed lodging in the Fleet'. She was not there long and Southampton, also serving a short sentence, had married her before their daughter Penelope was born. The marriage turned out well.

William Herbert, though pressed by the Fittons, 'utterly renounced marriage' with their reckless daughter. Unless he genuinely believed that the child was not his he was behaving callously. Poor Mall, who might have been a Countess, had no husband at all until she was married twice (and once in necessary haste) to country gentlemen of much less wealth and rank. On succeeding to his father's title the new Earl chose a wife of his own station and one with great expectations. She was Lady Mary Talbot, daughter of the Earl of Shrewsbury and co-heiress to his vast estates. She had no reputation as a beauty. Dr Rowse has described her as 'dwarfish and unattractive' and Clarendon said that Pembroke 'paid much too dear for his wife's fortune by taking her person into the bargain'. There was no surviving issue of the marriage.

Of its failure there were ugly rumours, but society gossip is not the best material for accurate history. One fact is plain. After his marriage Pembroke began to take seriously the duties of a rich and influential milord. None who knew him in youth would have expected him to become a Chancellor of the University of Oxford where his name abides in the College, originally Broadgates Hall, which was renamed in his honour. Unparalleled he could hardly be, but he had become a man of sufficient achievement and character to make the adjective not wholly ridiculous.

The Marriage Sonnets, set first in Thorpe's Quarto, are addressed to a handsome young man of high rank who is obstinately refusing to marry and get an heir. They could apply to Southampton if they were written before 1595 or to Pembroke if they came after that date. They must have been commissioned since it was no business of an outsider to interfere in the matrimonial arrangements of an aristocratic family. If these Sonnets were not asked for by a parent they are an impertinence. Southampton's mother knew that Shakespeare was a close friend of her son and received his patronage and could well have engaged him for that reason. Lady Pembroke, presiding over her Wilton Academe, herself a poetess among attending poets, would be expert in the choice of the talent most likely to execute superbly an embarrassing order of this kind.

The fact that one young man was asking another to take a wife discounts any unnatural affection between the two. Ardent homosexuals do not advocate bi-sexual love, which is a form of treachery to them, and the Sonnet (Number Twenty) which immediately follows the Marriage sequence expressly denies any suggestion of indulgence of that kind. There is no proof that William Herbert was that way prone. 'Inordinately given to women', said Clarendon. What the poet had to do was to dissuade the young lord from such a folly as later produced the Herbert–Fitton scandal and to get him decently and fruitfully married. That he did not succeed was not Shakespeare's fault. The reference to the mother's beauty agrees with Aubrey's description of 'Sidney's sister, Pembroke's mother':

> *Thou art thy mother's glass and she in thee*
> *Calls back the lovely April of her prime.*

The exact age of the Countess is unknown. She married in 1577 and thus would be beyond her lovely April in 1597 when the parental pressure was being applied to her nubile but reluctant son. The picture fits the young Mary Sidney and the great lady of Wilton both in the chronology and the compliment.

When the Queen died the victims of her anger could once more expect to live freely and prosperously. The new Scottish King prudently showed favour to those whom his predecessor had punished or degraded. Southampton, sent to the Tower for his share in the foolish and futile insurrection led by the Earl of Essex, came back to Court. So did the humiliated William Herbert, now the Third Earl of Pembroke, who was made a Knight of the Garter and given various posts of authority in the West Country. His brother Philip became a Knight of the Bath and a Gentleman of the Bedchamber. There was a Shakespearian association there since the actor, as a leading member of the King's Men, was a Groom in that apartment. If Shakespeare had been enraged by Pembroke's raid on Mall Fitton's affections he had made it plain in the Sonnets that the old wound, whoever inflicted it, quickly healed.

The two men had a chance to meet at Wilton, which was twice visited by the King in the summer and autumn of 1603. That was a Plague Year and London was a death-trap. There were thirty thousand deaths and the theatres were closed. Fortunately for the Establishment escape was easy. The seat of government was then easily loaded on a few coaches. A clustering swarm of

Civil Servants did not have to follow it. The Court headed for safety to the clean air of Wiltshire, staying at Salisbury and at Wilton with the Pembrokes. There was a royal arrival there in August and royal entertainment in December when a team of players, naturally the King's Men, were summoned from their suburban refuge at Mortlake to travel a hundred miles in mid-winter weather and present one play for a reward sufficient. The Chamber Account gives documentary evidence of this fact and there was mention of a fee of thirty pounds, but the name of the play is not stated.

The Victorian poet and Eton College master William Cory left a note indicating that it was *As You Like It*. This he had gathered from a Lady Herbert who told him of a letter, never printed, from Lady Pembroke to her son telling him to bring the King from Salisbury to see that comedy and adding, 'We have the man Shakespeare with us.' The letter has been searched for and never found. It may have been the invention of a house-proud Herbert eager to add to the history of Wilton, but I see no reason for discrediting the idea of Shakespeare as a guest. If he had pre-viously served Lady Pembroke by writing the Marriage Sonnets he was closely associated with the family. He had become the principal dramatist of the day. Lady Pembroke, so anxious to be surrounded by 'ingeniose persons', would have had in him the most ingenious of all, a prize lion of the Bankside forest for the collector of the Wilton Brains Trust.

That Shakespeare would be one of the King's Men invited to entertain the play-loving King and Queen is more than probable. He was still acting and some of his parts were important. He was to appear next year in Ben Jonson's *Sejanus* and in Jonson's Folio he is mentioned after Burbage as a leading member of the cast. So, as poet, supervisor as well as a refugee from the pestilence in London, he had sufficient cause to be working with his com-panions at Wilton, and would be very glad to be accepted in a house of distinguished and liberal patronage. In this case the visit was partly a royal Command. As a 'Groom of the Chamber' he would have to be included. He was also a possible player of Adam and supervisor of the production which had to be adapted to whatever great room was put at his disposal by the Pembrokes.

William Herbert had found life in London alluring. In Wiltshire he had a home and adjacent country described by Aubrey as 'an Arcadian place and a paradise'. But the paradise was a wilderness to the aspiring courtier. When driven from London by Queen Elizabeth he twice complained to Sir Robert Cecil of an enforced idleness at Wilton and bitter deprivation. Away from London, he said: 'I shall undoubtedly turn clown, for justice of the peace I can by no means frame unto and one of the two a man that lives in the country must be. If you mean to have a gamester of me, you were best by some means to get me from hence. For here there is no game known but trump; *primero* is a conjuring word.' Trump is defined in the *Oxford English Dictionary* as 'an obsolete card game sometimes known as ruff'; primero as 'a gambling card game in which four cards were dealt to each player, each having thrice its ordinary value'. The latter was better sport for those who liked to cut a dash and take a chance in Whitehall.

Pembroke had no heir to spend his boyhood in the great house and its park. There was one sickly child of his marriage who died in infancy. So the bereaved father proceeded to be a courtier on the fringe and sometimes near the centre of power, but never as close to King James as were his pet politicians, Villiers and Carr. It was an ugly world whose corridors were full of whispering malice and squalid intrigue. But Pembroke's integrity was not smirched. He took part in the expanding development of overseas trade and was a member of the Virginia Company in whose sometimes vexed fortunes and exacting problems he had a share with another Shakespeare patron, Southampton.

He was genuinely fond of the arts and of poetry in particular. He was a champion of George Herbert, a very different character from those to be met among the players and at the Court of King James. Izaak Walton recorded that Pembroke was influential in getting that pious and retiring poet made Public Orator at Cambridge. The King asked Pembroke if George was a friend and was told that the Earl did know him well and was a kinsman but 'loved him more for his learning and virtue than for that he was of his name and family'. James asked the Earl's leave 'that he might love him too for he took him to be the jewel of the University'. The loves of that curious King were assorted and sometimes deplorable, but in appreciating the grave and beautifully worded lines and tender piety of this country clergyman he was earning his reputation for wisdom as well as folly. George Herbert praised a cloistered goodness remote from the London so dear to Pembroke, but the latter 'prosecuted him with much favour' in finance for his parish church as well as in support for an academic honour.

For George Herbert there was as much goodness in a peaceful and pastoral isolation as there was for Wordsworth.

> *Sweet day, so cool, so calm, so bright!*
> *The bridal of the earth and sky—*
> *The dew shall weep thy fall to-night;*
> *For thou must die.*

> *Sweet rose, whose hue angry and brave*
> *Bids the rash gazer wipe his eye,*
> *Thy root is ever in its grave,*
> *And thou must die.*

> *Sweet spring, full of sweet days and roses,*
> *A box where sweets compacted lie,*
> *My music shows ye have your closes,*
> *And all must die.*

> *Only a sweet and virtuous soul,*
> *Like season'd timber, never gives;*
> *But though the whole world turn to coal,*
> *Then chiefly lives.*

Days in the country, 'cool, calm, and bright', were never enjoyed by William Herbert. But his width of appreciation is shown by his regard for a man of simple saintliness who could see heaven in a flower. The poet George Herbert was far removed from the sumptuous masques, the wild extravagances, the thrusting ambitions and rancorous animosities of the Court of King James in which Pembroke achieved success and presumably found intermittent satisfaction. In the midst of this he championed as patron the unworldly clergyman and more than once was bountiful to his parochial needs.

The Earl had a prominent place at the Coronation of King Charles I who, according to Aubrey, 'did love Wilton above all places and came thither every summer'. When Pembroke died without an heir in 1630 at the age of fifty, Philip succeeded him in the title and the estate. The King, said Aubrey, 'put him (the new Earl) on making this magnificent garden and grotto and to new building that side of the house that fronts the garden with two stately pavilions at each end, all *al Italiano*'. Philip, never so likeable a character as William, who began as a rake and ended as a man of culture and kindliness, found the post of Lord Chamberlain, in which he followed his brother, to be worrying. Theatrical affairs are always likely to be stormy, and their arbiters, as administrators of the Stage Censorship in subsequent centuries were to learn, cannot expect a tranquil life. His hot temper did not make for smooth dealing with disputes and his widow wrote after his death that he was no scholar, having spent only three months at Oxford, yet 'he was of a very quick apprehension, a sharp understanding, very crafty withal and of a discerning spirit, but extremely choleric by nature which was increased the more by the office of Lord Chamberlain to the King which he held many years'.

The woman who left that critical assessment was his second wife, Anne, Countess of Dorset. She had had twenty years experience of the quick apprehension and even hastier temper. Philip's first wife had been Lady Susan Vere, a sister of the Lady Bridget whom William had rejected and of the Lady Elizabeth whom Southampton had evaded. By Susan Philip had two sons. There was the desired heir to Wilton whom William's well-dowered but physically frail wife had failed to provide.

King James, uncouth himself, was not dismayed by Philip's

choleric pugnacity. (He had come to blows with Southampton at a game of tennis in which rackets became weapons of assault.) The royal favour was generously shown. Philip was soon awarded the Earldom and the castle of Montgomery. Later on he succeeded in two offices his temperate brother who healed more quarrels than he caused. He was both Lord Chamberlain and Chancellor of Oxford University, though little suited to the second honour. If he felt any debt to the Stuarts he forgot it. After violent quarrels with King Charles he joined the Parliamentarians in the Civil War. Just before his own death in 1650 he saw the doomed King walk into Whitehall to meet the executioner. He had the decency to avoid seeing the horror of the severed head.

His widow added to her observations on a volatile, shrewd, and cunning character a kindly final tribute. He was, she concluded, 'one of the greatest noblemen of his time in England in all respects and was generally throughout the realm very much beloved'.

The 'generally' is nonsensical. At the end of his life he was loathed by the Royalists. He had always made bitter enemies. Oxford accepted him unwillingly. The learned thought him ignorant and the good-mannered thought him a boor. But he had won his niche of honour in the most famous of all English books of poetry and plays. He cannot have been completely crude since he had shared William's admiration for Shakespeare and showed generosity in the bestowal of the unspecified favours. By no means an Incomparable, he did not add to the renown of Wilton as an Academe, but as a Paradise he preserved it and, after a destructive fire in 1647, he consulted one truly beyond compare, Inigo Jones, supreme native master of the classical, Palladian style which he had imported and adapted to the English cities and country landscapes. Inigo was too old to do the practical work of rebuilding and called in his assistant, Webb. The result, especially the south front of the mansion, has been acclaimed as a masterpiece. Sir John Summerson has called it 'a composition of perfect balance'. That is exactly the praise due to one of Shakespeare's finest Sonnets which may have been evoked fifty years earlier

by the discerning choice of the Countess. She was an acknowledged Tudor Paragon whatever the validity of the adjective
bestowed upon her sons in the dedication of the First Folio.

The behaviour and achievements of the Brethren, whatever
epithets be applied to them, reveal the strangely contrasted
qualities, the delicacy of taste and the coarseness of conduct, the
noble munificence and the shabby matrimonial money-grubbing
of 'Jacobethan' England. For the noblemen a policy of 'Safety
First' had no attraction. To gain was to spend. The Third Earl of
Pembroke began by defying his father and enraging his Queen.
To this audacity he added the physical gallantry which made him,
like his brother Philip, a dashing champion of the tilt-yard.
Southampton risked his head for a hopeless cause and was twice
gaoled by his Queen. To be an active courtier in the reign of King
James was to swim in a vortex of intrigue where failure to take
the right line could be ruinous and even lethal. And how could
anyone be sure of the right move on that chequer-board of
supreme power with a monarch so shifty and capricious? It is
hard to understand these ardent spirits who disdained caution in
so many hazardous ventures and yet married for money with a
cold calculation more proper to a scheming skinflint in a petty-
bourgeois family.

Then, having acquired their fortunes, they were ready to
squander them in foppery, display, and dissipation. But their
bounty could be as remarkable as their self-indulgence. They were
fascinated by the bright and glittering thing, by the gold of a
bride, by the sumptuous extravagance of a Court Masque, and,
to their eternal credit, by the treasure of the English language and
of the poets who wrought it into exquisite patterns. Even Philip
Herbert, turbulent and widely removed from his maternal
Academe, was no 'clod without a spark'. He too could discern
the excellence of a poet, an actor, and a playwright.

On the edge of this whirlpool of dangerous waters in Whitehall
was the Shakespeare who, as always, could see both sides of a
case. The History plays and the long political oration delivered by
Ulysses in *Troilus and Cressida* attest his belief that a disciplined

rule of order was essential to a community and that to attain this escape from the murderous turmoil of the old baronial wars there must be acceptance of what he called Degree. He respected rank in the social structure; that was a reasoned belief in the stability which it maintained. But inside him was an impulsive sympathy for the natural, boisterous, and even anarchic side of human nature. He became, as he knew, too fond of his own Falstaff and had to contrive the old rogue's humiliation in order that contempt of the law should not seem to prevail.

So we get the clash of loyalties in his work. The Sonnets declare the deferential man, humble in the presence of Degree. In the plays the conservative mind of Shakespeare jostles with the instincts of the radical. Here are both the angry and the laughing dramatist, stripping power of its pretences and mocking the absurdities of authority misused. As a servant of the Crown in two companies of players attached to the Court he had seen it all, the ups and downs of great ones and the revenges of whirligig Time.

In the case of Southampton and the two Herberts he had watched characteristic careers of his age, noting their headstrong faults and gratefully aware of their generosity. By one of time's ironies the three Earls have still an abiding place in the researches and biographies of the scholars. The Folio's dedication has preserved the fame of the Wilton brothers with an adjective which only a superman could justify. They survive in the chronicles because they were patrons of a poet who was himself an Incomparable.

CHAPTER XI

The Role of Berowne

ACTORS NATURALLY have parts in which they are said 'to see themselves'. An actor who is also an author is therefore inclined to create roles of that kind and is in a strong position to suit himself. I believe that in his early years Shakespeare did follow that inclination. Then was his chance. Later he could not do so. When Burbage had become established as their acknowledged leader by the Chamberlain's Men and as the applauded favourite of their public the urgent need was to keep him supplied with the good, fat parts which he could turn to such profitable use. There were the other players with their various skills and preferences for whom a series of character parts had to be included.

Shakespeare became ever busier with his pen and more and more needed in the conferences of the Sharers and for the guidance of rehearsals. Nobody with acting in the blood can be content with a long succession of 'bit parts'. Naturally he yearned to be constantly and importantly on the stage and he denied himself to suit his colleagues. But at one time, as I see it, he had seen himself as no minor shadow, limited to the tottering Adam or the briefly eloquent Ghost. Once he drew in full size a young man, clever but contemptuous of book-learning, quick to fall in love, fertile both in praise of its raptures and in description of its torment, a man of wit, a man of charm, and the victim of a dark beauty who was as fickle as she was commanding. In short, a man like himself.

That man was Berowne in *Love's Labour's Lost*, Berowne the infatuated poet and sonneteer. He not only writes in that form but speaks Sonnets embedded in Shakespeare's text. The pains of what is now frequently called 'a love–hate relationship' with his enchantress are as explicit in the play as they are in the final section of Thorpe's Quarto which, mysteriously emerging in

1608, revealed the emotional fever of an earlier decade. If, as Milton suggested and Browning queried, Shakespeare unlocked his heart in his Sonnets he had done some rattling of the key when he wrote *Love's Labour's Lost* and set Berowne railing at an irresistible wanton.

That, having seen himself as Berowne, he ever did get the chance to play the part is a matter of conjecture. That he had himself in mind is an idea abundantly suggested, and I think confirmed, in the play. For that reason I have found in this comedy a perpetual fascination and have thought that a close inspection of its origin and the mood behind its composition was relevant to a book on Shakespeare as a player among players and as one who wrote primarily for speakers and listeners, not for readers.

The academic commentators editing *Love's Labour's Lost* have said little of the fact that it is unique in one way; the scene never changes. It starts in the Park of the King of Navarre and emparked we remain throughout. It is the only play of Shakespeare's which never moves indoors. We think of *As You Like It* as a pastoral and sylvan play, but it has scenes in the Duke's palace. In *Twelfth Night* more happens in Olivia's house than in her garden. In *L.L.L.*, an abbreviation to be used henceforward for convenience, a tent is erected. That is a pavilion for the Princess of France before the long second scene of Act V, but the action continues in front of it to the end. Accordingly it is the most suitable of plays for performance on a lawn by those willing to take a chance with the weather. That is always a dangerous risk in the climate of an English summer, but with luck it can be a rich experience.

I have been fortunate. My first view of the play was in the garden of Wadham College, Oxford, to which I was invited as the London critic of the *Manchester Guardian*. It was a perfect site, with grey walls about to remind us that the King had a palace. In those quieter years there was no interruption by 'noises without'—or above. There were the lawns, the trees, and the flowerbeds to give Navarre full scenic honours. The night, following a radiant sunset, was dry, calm and warm. It is a play for 'brisky juvenals' and youth trod its measure. The members of the Oxford University

Dramatic Society caught the right spirit of pastoral hey-go-mad and aristocratic escapade. The drolls and yokels were well cast.

I remember vividly the performance of the small part of Constable Dull. The player was named in the programme as G. E. Williams, Christ Church. He was soon to become and remain famous as Emlyn Williams. The O.U.D.S. did not then include members of the Women's Colleges and professional actresses were invited to play the feminine roles. In this case Veronica Turleigh, in the April of her stage-life soon to reach the richness of summer, came from J. B. Fagan's Company to play the ebon Rosalind; Berowne's enchantress took the eye and the ear in the swift exchange of wit and wantonness like volleying at lawn tennis. Across the serenity of an ideal Oxford evening flew the winged words.

My second critical attendance was also of an amateur performance. There is a kind of bubbling amateurishness in much of *L.L.L.* and it is essential that the performers should be enjoying themselves and not clouded by the cares of the professional who is worrying about reputation and 'the notices'. I was invited to visit a country house at Rogate in Sussex. I was in luck again. There was a perfect summer afternoon and a perfect site, a clearance in a wood with sunshine filtering through from an unclouded sky. Since the players were of Horseback Hall quality they brought their mounts with them. The light cavalry of Navarre behaved admirably. This was no exhibitionist intrusion. There is horsemanship in the text (IV, i), but Shakespeare, with his mind on indoor performance to follow, did not necessitate riding in full view. But the equestrian arrivals in the Rogate coppice were an added pleasure to an occasion in which the amateur actors were true to the proper meaning of that adjective. They were loving their enterprise. They were also unexpectedly competent.

How wrong can professional directors go? In the last production which I saw at Stratford-upon-Avon the scene suggested a winter in Norway. Even in Sir Laurence Olivier's much livelier presentation at the Old Vic in 1968 the trees were naked timber, as though the palace of Navarre was in the dark heart of a stark forest where no grass grew and no bird sang. The hints of sunshine were few. Here was no site for a picnic with a feast of words or a romp of quipping lovers. The Olivier version had ingenious touches of comedy and the ladies the right dancing grace, but the players did not seem to be enjoying themselves. This comedy is more than a verbal ballet: it is a young poet's play about young men larking. The lovers sometimes groan, but they are mainly involved in a gambol.

It is a reasonable supposition that *L.L.L.*, being continuously an al fresco jaunt, was written for a nobleman's park or the lawn of one of the Inns of Court. The date of its first composition is uncertain. It could go back to the years of Shakespeare's profitable attachment to the Earl of Southampton who may have bidden his much-liked poet of high promise to supply a gay occasion for his country house in Hampshire or for the 'termers' of Gray's Inn whose appetite for plays was keen and whose percipient relish of mannered and intricate word-juggling could be assumed.

There are many reasons for thinking that *L.L.L.* is the most personal of Shakespeare's plays. To those curious about the secrets of the private life of this supreme but elusive genius it is therefore especially alluring. Since detective novels and 'whodunit' plays are immensely popular it should have a particular attraction at the present time. It is full of topical references. For that reason it has been industriously scrutinised under the microscopes of academic scholarship.

Yet nothing is certainly established except that it was first published in Quarto form in 1598 and acted before Queen Elizabeth at the Christmas revels of that year. It is certain that the text is not that of the original version. It is described as 'A Pleasant Conceited Comedy newly corrected and augmented by W. Shakespere'. It was 'imprinted by W.W. for Cuthbert Burby'. W.W., William White, later printed six more Shakespeare Quartos. The 'newly' is important because it indicates that the author had been recently revising and inserting. Why otherwise is the new timing of the augmentation mentioned?

We know nothing of the first version, perhaps much earlier,

which the author had decided to be in need of correction and addition. Certainly in style and vocabulary it is closely connected with the Sonnets, but since there is no agreement about the date of the Sonnets or the man called 'the lovely boy' to whom they were written that does not help us. Six plays accepted as Shakespeare's work by the Editors of the First Folio had been printed in Quarto before *L.L.L.* Only in 1598 was the author's name mentioned on the title page. If Shakespeare's name was increasingly known not only in the theatre but in the news and gossip of the day the naming of the author might bring in more customers for the new book on Cuthbert Burby's counter.

The recommendation of the play is justified. To use Bernard Shaw's label it can be set among Shakespeare's 'Plays Pleasant'. It ends with a funeral note but throughout it has mixed clowning with exchanges of wit in the punning word-play called conceits. These were relished by the Elizabethans but are often tedious to us because the meanings of the words have changed, the topical allusions are cryptic, and puns, dear to the Victorians, are now out of fashion. A string of epigrams made fashionable by Oscar Wilde and kept up in the early comedies of Somerset Maugham was one successor of the Shakespearian conceit. America introduced the rougher wisecrack, which was farther still from the intricate verbal fencing of the fifteen-nineties.

L.L.L. is so very much a comedy written for a social 'set' that, despite the broad clowning in some episodes, it was unlikely to be widely popular. Burby's First Quarto mentions only a Command Performance whereas the First Quarto of *Romeo and Juliet* stated that 'it hath been often (with great applause) plaid publiquely'. The booksellers of the Quartos usually mentioned a good public reception. There was another private performance of *L.L.L.* in 1605. Burbage recommended it for the entertainment of James I's Danish Queen, a great lover of plays and masques, holding out the hope that for wit and mirth 'it will please her exceedingly'. That it did later on have some public appeal is shown in the title page of the Second Quarto published in 1631 in which it is described as 'acted by His Majesty's Servants' at the

Blackfriars and the Globe. There is no mention of frequency or great applause. That it did better at the roofed and intimate Blackfriars play-house, which had a wealthy and 'smart set' audience, than in the more popular, less comfortable, and financially less profitable Globe, is a reasonable surmise.

But after that came two centuries of total absence from the stage. At Covent Garden in 1839 Charles Matthews with Madame Vestris attempted it. So did Samuel Phelps in 1857. Stratford-upon-Avon in 1885 and 1907 gave it the tribute of brief performance. Slowly it came back to life. Now it is quite frequently to be seen and the most eminent directors, including Tyrone Guthrie and Peter Brook, have exercised their talent in re-animating the antics, humours, and, with less ease, the conceits long believed to be dead matter. I particularly enjoyed a revival for the Old Vic Company by Hugh Hunt in 1951. This had a sparkling vivacity, the right dancing movement and the lyrical touch. Dr Dover Wilson in his book on *The Happy Comedies*, published in 1964, recorded his complete conversion from the old belief that *L.L.L.* is unactable. Tyrone Guthrie's staging at the Old Vic in 1937 had been his persuader and he has rightly pointed out that Granville-Barker's encouraging and brilliant Preface, written in 1927, had been a valuable aid and stimulus to those who put new life into the old bones so long relegated to the charnel-house.

A play written and perhaps commissioned to amuse a group on a certain occasion inevitably contained topical allusion and portraiture, even caricaturing, of persons known to its members. The interpretations have been many and assorted. Armado was described in detail:

> *a refinèd traveller of Spain—*
> *A man in all the world's new fashion planted,*
> *That hath a mint of phrases in his brain:*
> *One who the music of his own vain tongue*
> *Doth ravish like enchanting harmony.*
>
> *How you delight, my lords, I know not, I,*
> *But I protest I love to hear him lie.*

Shakespeare was telling them what to expect, says Dover Wilson in his Preface to the Cambridge University Press Edition of *L.L.L.*, 'namely the dandy and planter of Virginia, spinner of travellers' tales, whose poem "The Lie" must have been known to all'. The pedantic school-master Holofernes Dr Wilson identifies not, as has often been done, with Southampton's tutor, the erudite John Florio, but with Raleigh's associate Thomas Harriot. Variations on this view are to be found in the Arden Edition edited by Richard David. But it is not my business, nor within my smaller range of Elizabethan specialism, to add to that debate.

Much less has been said about the relevance of the play's principal male character, Berowne, in whom I believe Shakespeare was instinctively and perhaps deliberately shadowing himself. When the Princess of France and her Ladies have arrived at Navarre the Princess inquires about 'the vow-fellows with this virtuous Duke' who have pledged themselves to three years ascetic study during which time 'no woman may approach his silent court'. After the keen wits and other qualities of the Lords Longaville and Dumain have been discussed by the Ladies in Waiting, Maria and Katharine, the dark lady Rosaline gives her opinion of Berowne, who had previously danced with her in Brabant.

> *Berowne they call him; but a merrier man,*
> *Within the limit of becoming mirth,*
> *I never spent an hour's talk withal:*
> *His eye begets occasion for his wit;*
> *For every object that the one doth catch,*
> *The other turns to a mirth-moving jest,*
> *Which his fair tongue—conceit's expositor—*
> *Delivers in such apt and gracious words,*
> *That aged ears play truant at his tales,*
> *And younger hearings are quite ravished;*
> *So sweet and voluble is his discourse.*

If Shakespeare was seeing himself as this exemplary master of keen observation and lively discourse he can be accused of vanity. But, as Bernard Shaw pointed out in his Preface to *The Dark Lady of the Sonnets*, Shakespeare in his sonneteering vein was frankly self-confident and self-assertive, proclaiming that neither marble nor gold would outlive 'this powerful rhyme'. As Shaw put it, 'The timid cough of the minor poet was never heard from him.' If Rosaline's praise of Berowne for apt and gracious words was not a piece of self-description it could very well be a laughing statement of what he hoped to be and was well on his way to becoming.

That is a minor point. More significant are Berowne's clearly stated opinions. Truth, he maintains in his explicit speech about learning (I, i, lines 74 onwards), is not to be discovered by painful poring over books. There in sonnet form speaks the young man who had missed a university career and was rudely put in his place by one and perhaps more of the less successful dramatists who had arrived with Oxford and Cambridge degrees to scratch a living in the London Theatres.

> *Study is like the heaven's glorious sun,*
> *That will not be deep-search'd with saucy looks:*
> *Small have continual plodders ever won,*
> *Save base authority from others' books.*
> *These earthly godfathers of heaven's lights,*
> *That give a name to every fixed star,*
> *Have no more profit of their shining nights*
> *Then those that walk and wot not what they are.*
> *Too much to know, is to know naught but fame;*
> *And every godfather can give a name.*

Base authority! Pedantic name-dropping! Shakespeare was not accepting accuracy and omniscience as necessary virtues in a poet and artist. To him starlight was the illumination of loving hours and not a theme for displaying an astronomical knowledge and its vocabulary. He used history-books as their master and not their slave. As the King shrewdly says, 'How well he's read who reasons against reading!' Berowne jestingly admits to being what Matthew Arnold called a Philistine:

> *I have for barbarism spoke more*
> *Than for that angel knowledge you can say.*

As Berowne he put common sense and a wide appreciation of life before the self-satisfaction of the scholar academically equipped.

Berowne is a French lord with his feet on English ground. It was my good fortune on a few occasions to find that 'the soft eye-music of slow-waving boughs', to use a line of Wordsworth's, could be this play's best accompaniment if one did not have to make a sudden bolt for shelter under rain-pattering leaves. There is a melodic quality in the speech-rhythm and the point-counter-point of the dialogue when the conceits are being exchanged. A more important excuse for a summer-time production on the grass is the constant presence in the text of rural sights and sounds.

Amid all the urban sophistication of the French lords and ladies there are recurrent memories of the English countryside which was never far out of Shakespeare's mind and affections. The parting song, so far separated from the aristocratic society who provide the principal characters and the comedy of their broken pledge, come straight from a Warwickshire boyhood with its farmhouse memories of bright, spring days and bitter winter mornings. What have Dick the shepherd and Tom the wood-cutter to do with Navarre? What red-nosed, frost-nipped Marian and greasy Joan, the latter at least warm but hard at work in the kitchen where she sweats over her steaming pots?

In any spring-time of France there would be 'meadows painted with delight' and the repetitive conjugal warning of the cuckoo. But the flowers, daisies pied and violets blue, white lady-smocks and yellow cuckoo-buds, are such as were plentiful on Avonside. Navarre is far away. There is no mention of the alien or the rarer blossoms. There are no lilies of France where the maids are bleaching their summer frocks. In the play's background are children who whip their gigs (tops) while their seniors play push-pin. There are rooks and daws in the park, swerving and cawing over the oaks, cedars, and sycamores where the owls await the time for predatory flight and melancholy sound. Costard and Jacquenetta are cousins of the 'country copulatives' of *As You Like It* and the school-master Holofernes, who teaches girls as well as boys (a point to be noticed by those who think that all the women in Shakespeare's life were illiterate), is as much an English pedagogue as any who ever set the boys yawning in an Elizabethan Grammar School with its heavily classical curriculum. Today's audience may think there is too much of this pedant's hard-worked latinity. But the dramatist was remembering Latin lessons that went on and on.

There are always the two Shakespeares. There is the man with country memories which are apt to recur in most unlikely places to provide a simile. (In Antony's maritime war Cleopatra, betraying him by putting her fleet in flight, is likened to a farmer's skittish animal on heat or stung by a gad-fly with 'the breeze upon her like a cow in June'.) There is the man about London, the player whose work takes him to the fringe of Court life, dazzled by the allure of feminine beauty or bantering wit. In *L.L.L.* Court and countryside mingle their language, their silks and their homespun. The poet, contemptuous of the scholar's learning, remembers his classics, not the cumbrous lore of Holofernes but the legends of labouring Hercules and Argus with his hundred eyes. So Berowne, with that soaring eloquence which had made *Romeo and Juliet* as lyrical as tragical, pours out the praise of love. He is in full cry in the long salute to amorous ecstasy in Act IV, Scene iii. The text is confused by repetition of some of the finest lines which indicates a passage rewritten or carelessly printed in the 'augmentation' of 1598.

> *But love, first learned in a lady's eyes,*
> *Lives not alone immured in the brain;*
> *But, with the motion of all elements,*
> *Courses as swift as thought in every power,*
> *And gives to every power a double power,*
> *Above their functions and their offices.*

> *It adds a precious seeing to the eye;*
> *A lover's eyes will gaze an eagle blind;*
> *A lover's ear will hear the lowest sound,*
> *When the suspicious head of theft is stopp'd:*
> *If that she learn not of her eye to look:*
> *No face is fair that is not full so black.*

Previous to the praise of love-light in the eyes there had been elaborate quipping over dark and fair. It may seem tiresome now, but why was it written unless a select audience enjoyed a reference to a Dark Lady who was in the Court news?

KING:　　　　*O paradox! Black is the badge of hell,*
　　　　　　　The hue of dungeons and the stole of night;
　　　　　　　And beauty's crest becomes the heavens well.

BEROWNE:　　*Devils soonest tempt, resembling spirits of light.*
　　　　　　　O, if in black my lady's brows be deck'd,
　　　　　　　　It mourns that painting and usurping hair
　　　　　　　Should ravish doters with a false aspect;
　　　　　　　　And therefore is she born to make black fair.
　　　　　　　Her favour turns the fashion of the days,
　　　　　　　　For native blood is counted painting now;
　　　　　　　And therefore red, that would avoid dispraise,
　　　　　　　　Paints itself black, to imitate her brow.

DUMAINE:　　*To look like her are chimney-sweepers black.*

LONGAVILLE:　*And since her time are colliers counted bright.*

KING:　　　　*And Ethiopes of their sweet complexion crack.*

DUMAINE:　　*Dark needs no candles now, for dark is light.*

BEROWNE:　　*I'll prove her fair, or talk till doomsday here.*

This is repeated, in almost exactly the same language, in Sonnets 127 and 132, with further insistence in both on the union of black with mourning, a point made by Berowne. At every turn in the texts of *L.L.L.* and the Sonnets it becomes increasingly tempting to suppose that Shakespeare is speaking as Berowne. There is no evidence that he ever played the part himself. But he may have done when it was first written. The fact that Burbage recommended the play for the private performance of 1605 can suggest that he had by then taken over the role. An actor would naturally recommend a piece that had a rewarding part for him.

But there had been that early version, dated by some at 1593. I can imagine an open-air performance out of London at a time when the disastrous epidemic of plague had made a country house a valuable refuge. Suppose Southampton wanted and ordered a comedy for his guests. Shakespeare was always eager to act. Here was a chance to show that he could be protagonist as well as playwright. Berowne is speaking Shakespeare's thoughts. How agreeable then to speak what he had written. But I think that the beautiful Rosaline only became the dark and wanton charmer in the rewritten and enlarged version of 1598. By that time Shakespeare had met the woman who was to entrance, betray, and infuriate.

In 1597 there had come to the Court of Queen Elizabeth in the privileged position of a Maid of Honour a girl of seventeen or eighteen. Her name was Mary Fitton, elder daughter of a knight and landowner in Cheshire. She presumably obtained this post because she was the ward of Sir William Knollys who had been appointed Comptroller of the Royal Household in 1596. Knollys was a married man of fifty and, at the Queen's side, had a reputation to maintain. Supposed by the Fittons to guard her from the young 'wolves' about the Court, and promising to be thus protective, he was an odd choice for that office. He was not too old to be lecherous. Mary Fitton, generally known as Mall, at once fascinated him, as she did others. We know much about this from the letters which he wrote with astonishing frankness to Mall's mother and younger sister. These were preserved in the family archives of the Newdigate–Newdegate family and published in 1897. The Queen held extremely strict views about the behaviour at Whitehall. Knollys had to be careful. To be caught in bed with a Maid of Honour would be fatal to his career. He longed to marry Mall but could only do so if his wife died. The shameless Comptroller admitted longing for that to happen.

The news of this ugly infatuation is not based on gossip. The Comptroller's letters to the Fitton family are explicit. That Mall,

a lively girl in her teens, would have accepted him is most unlikely. Around her was 'metal more attractive'. She was high in
the Queen's favour for some years. There is contemporary evidence that, when the other Maids were in their own apartments
at night, she liked to 'frisk and hey about'. It is certain that she was
seduced by (or seduced) Lord William Herbert, heir to the Earldom of Pembroke and the great house of Wilton, born in 1580,
and bore him an illegitimate and short-lived son early in 1601. The
Queen would not tolerate such behaviour and Mall was dismissed
from Court and went back to Cheshire. Herbert, who was sent
to the Fleet Prison, refused to marry her. He may have argued
that the child was not certainly his and that Mall had other lovers.
Dr Leslie Hotson has convincingly shown that she and Knollys
were the talk of the town and that he was publicly ridiculed by the
sellers of ballads in the streets. He shows that Knollys was carica-
tured as Malvolio in *Twelfth Night* and that Sir Toby Belch alludes
to Mall's disgrace when he asks why is Mistress Mall's picture
hidden and left in the dust (I, iii). He can only be referring to the
scandal of the day in London. The remark, with its introduction
of a well-known girl's name, has no possible relevance to Illyria.

It may naturally be asked what all this has to do with *L.L.L.*
The answer is that Mall's name is indirectly introduced into a
speech of Berowne's in which he mentions his own compositions
as a poet and a lover and his use of a Sonnet to convey his feelings
(IV, i). Here is a point of great significance which I had previously
and stupidly overlooked when I wrote a book on *The Women in
Shakespeare's Life*. My awareness of it was caused by a letter on
this topic from Sir Alan Lascelles to whom I am most grateful.
Berowne's words (IV, iii) are:

'The king he is hunting the deer; I am coursing myself; they have
pitch'd a toil; I am toiling in a pitch,—pitch that defiles: defile! a
foul word. Well, set thee down, sorrow! for so they say the fool
said, and so say I, and I the fool: well proved, wit! By the Lord,
this love is as mad as Ajax: it kills sheep; it kills me, I a sheep:
well proved again o' my side! I will not love: If I do, hang me;

i' faith, I will not. O, but her eye,—by this light, but for her eye,
I would not love her; yes, for her two eyes. Well, I do nothing
in the world but lie, and lie in my throat. By heaven, I do love:
and it hath taught me to rime, and to be mallicholie; and here is
part of my rime, and here my mallicholie. Well, she hath one o'
my sonnets already: the clown bore it, the fool sent it, and the
lady hath it:'

Here again are the mesmeric eyes. Here too there is the application of pitch-black colour to the woman who snares him in her
'toil'. 'Two pitch-balls stuck in her face for eyes.' Why is the
simile repeated if Berowne is not obsessed by this vision which
keeps reappearing in the language of the play? The word-play on
light and dark is incessant even when Rosaline and Katharine
are twitting each other at the beginning of Act V, Scene ii. What
is most striking in Berowne's speech in prose, just quoted, is the
conversion of 'melancholy' into 'mallicholie'. Melancholy, with
the alternative spelling melancholie, is a word used four other
times in L.L.L. Once it is spoken by the King, twice by the
love-sick Armado, and once by Katharine. In all four cases the
form of the word in the First Quarto and First Folio is normal.
Only when Berowne is the speaker and Rosaline the subject of
his despair does it become Mallicholie.

Nearly all subsequent editors, not spotting this curious fact
and not suspecting the presence of a real woman's name, altered
the noun to Melancholy. Both Dover Wilson (Cambridge edition)
and Richard David (Arden) adopted the usual emendation. One
editor who did keep Mallicholie, only substituting 'y' for 'ie',
was A. H. Bullen of the Shakespeare Head Press. His text was
used in Odhams' Omnibus publication of *The Works of William
Shakespeare Gathered into One Volume*. There I came across it.

It seems to me most unlikely that the appearance of Mallicholie,
here and here alone in the play, is a mere coincidence. Shakespeare
must have written Mallicholie in the 'augmented' version of 1598,
which was also the year of the command performance before the
Queen. It is probable that the Maids of Honour would be in

attendance, particularly Mall Fitton with her taste for a frisk. Shakespeare's company, known as the Lord Chamberlain's Men, were the Queen's favourites. That Mall was familiar with them is shown by the dedication of a book written in 1601 by Will Kempe, the chief clown and for some years a leading member, along with Shakespeare and Burbage, of this 'fellowship' of players.

Kempe quarrelled with his colleagues, perhaps because he gagged too much and was the target of Hamlet's censure of those who spoke 'more than is set down for them'. A frisky fellow, he called attention to himself by dancing a morris from London to Norwich and then wrote his own chronicle of that feat. He dedicated this to Mistress Ann Fitton and called her a Maid of Honour to the Queen, which position Ann, rarely a visitor to London, never held. It seems Kempe must have mistaken the Christian name. Either way it is plain that one of the Fitton girls was on easy terms with the actors.

Since Ann was a much less 'hey about' type, stayed mainly in the country, and had married happily into the Newdigate family before Kempe's escapade took place, I envisage a Court performance with Mall Fitton, already with a reputation for high-spirited charm, in attendance. Berowne, if Burbage took the part, is instructed by the author to stress the first syllable and perhaps point it with a look in her direction. Her gaiety being known to the Whitehall gossips in the audience, there would be a sly jest here for those in the know. Of course that is fancy, but fancy is sometimes factual. Without Shakespeare having Mall in mind I cannot understand the alteration of 'melancholie' into 'mallicholie' in one passage only. The printer would not have invented that, since he printed 'melancholie' elsewhere. It must have been in Shakespeare's script and put there for the benefit of those now called 'In People'.

The identification of both Shakespeare's Rosaline and the lost love of the Sonnets with Mall Fitton has been dismissed because a family portrait of the young lady from Cheshire presents her as a brunette. It is curious, however, that the reproduction in black and white in *Gossip from a Muniment Room* makes her hair and eyes as black as Berowne's pitch. If Mall's colouring was dark, the story fits in with the view, strongly argued by Dover Wilson, that Lord William Herbert was the recipient of the Male Sonnets. As I see it, in 1598 Mall has been two years cutting a dash at Court. There, on the actor's fringe of the royal revels, Shakespeare had seen her, met her, and been entranced. Herbert, then seventeen, came to Court in 1597. At some time in the next two years he too is fascinated and outshines Shakespeare in those much-mentioned eyes. He was an heir to an earldom and a great country mansion as well as, in Clarendon's words, 'inordinately given to women'; the highly-sexed and socially ambitious girl might well be inordinately given to him. Then came the scandal and the disaster to both of them.

When Bernard Shaw made Mall the central figure of his one-act play *The Dark Lady of the Sonnets* he admitted in his Preface that the discovery of the portrait made things difficult for Thomas Tyler, Frank Harris, and the early supporters of the Fitton theory. He suggested that when Mall sat for her picture she might have dyed her hair because then 'black hair was unpopular as red hair was in the early days of Queen Victoria'. The red-headed Gloriana had set the fashion for that modish tint in 'woman's crown of glory'. Fanciful again. With that we must leave Berowne and the cause of his Mallicholie.

But, whoever the woman was, Shakespeare was putting a lot of himself into the Sonnet-maker at the Court of Navarre and a lot of the Dark Lady into Rosaline. He also had something to say of his professional life as a man of words. Rewriting his second draft of the play he realised that his early style, precious and euphuistic in its continued complexity, was out of date. He had learned in his years of steady and triumphant play-writing that the public preferred a simpler kind of dialogue and less elaboration of a phrase. So he now confessed his past error and his resolve to be no longer the 'clever Dick' (or Will) aping fashion and nimbly throwing 'conceits' into the air like the plates tossed by a stage juggler. Therefore Berowne, declaring his purpose, again in sonnet form, vows to abandon

Taffeta phrases, silken terms precise,
  Three-pil'd hyperboles, spruce affectation,
Figures pedantical; these summer-flies
  Have blown me full of maggot ostentation:
I do forswear them; and I here protest,
  By this white glove,—how white the hand, God knows!—
Henceforce my wooing mind shall be express'd
  In russet yeas and honest kersey noes.

Rosaline has been called 'a whitely wanton'. Berowne swears with special emphasis on the whiteness of her hand. Then he goes on to his inescapable mention of eyes, now described as infecting him with the plague of love. In the Sonnets Shakespeare, not writing, as he then thought, for the public ear or eye, was explicit about his inner life. In no other play did he tell us so much about himself.

CHAPTER XII

Then and Now

WHEN SHAKESPEARE came to London a well-organized company of actors with a steady and continuing membership was a novelty in English life. A wayward occupation was being stabilised. Before that the Court Jesters, the drolls and clowns delighting the public, the University amateurs of whom the young Polonius seems to have been one, and the devoted, happy, and possibly crude performers in the cycles of the Miracle plays had added in their various styles to the colour and vitality of urban and village society. When the protection of the Patrons legalised the work of the mummers and raised their status there was created a new profession which trained, rehearsed and disciplined its entrants from boyhood to maturity. These soon found a ready and rewarding public of sufficient size and constancy to yield more than a bare and uncertain living.

The players had enemies on all sides. The Puritans called them caterpillars devastating the morals of the community and wanton scoundrels growing fit on filth. Some writers and poets to whom the actors brought a market were jealous of the applause they won and cursed them as conceited upstarts who were growing too big for their buskins. According to the writer of the tract on Ratsey and his pranks, issued in 1605, that highwayman had grumbled at their alleged prosperity and social ambitions. He said that 'when the actors felt their purses well-lined' they bought 'some place or lordship in the country' which brought 'dignity or reputation'. 'And in this presage and prophetical humour of mine', Ratsey is supposed to have said, 'Kneel down, Rise up, Sir Simon Two-and-a-Half Shares, thou art now one of my knights and the first knight that was ever a player in England.'

The genial rogue's mockery had some basis of reality in the

rise from vagabondage to home-building and house owning, but
he anticipated the accolade by nearly three hundred years. The
first theatrical knighthood was that of Sir Henry Irving in 1895.
Now titles are a familiar tribute to those, once 'harlotry players',
who have added responsibility as leaders of companies to their
possession of exceptional talents. The Dames have rightly joined
the Sirs. But during the centuries before the royal salute to Irving
the social ranking of the actors had not greatly differed from its
condition in Shakespeare's time. Those who drew a fashionable
audience in London and the big cities could prosper and have
fine houses in and out of town. They were accepted by the
Georgian milords to direct amateur theatricals in their mansions;
they could join the company of the wits in coffee-houses and at
dinners. That was the life enjoyed by Garrick, who was never
Sir David.

In Victorian society there was a renewal of the Puritan suspicion
of those whom some pious rustics called 'the pomping folk'. When
Irving came out of a counting house to steady toil with a stock
company on tour and when Ellen Terry, whose family had climbed
with difficulty from such 'life on the road' as Dickens inimitably
described in his portraiture of the Crummles family, became a
child actress it was the opinion of 'nice people' that it was not
'nice' to be a player. It was held that a self-respecting man or
woman should be better engaged than in a game of 'let's pretend'.
A powerful actor or a master of light comedy was the idol of a
limited Victorian public, but his occupation was one which 'a
good family' would not deem suitable for a son with a respectable
profession to follow, and still less for a daughter. The latter, with
no occupation ahead of her except as a badly paid teacher or a
governess living half-way between the drawing-room and the
servants' hall, was expected to devote her charms and accomplish-
ments to finding the right and reputable husband.

Some girls broke away, even from clerical homes. The daughters
of the Reverend Prebendary Barnes of Exeter took the stage as
Violet and Irene Vanbrugh in the well-respected company of
Sarah Thorne at Margate in 1886 and 1888. They had triumphant

lives. Irene became a Dame in 1941. Dame Sybil Thorndike came from a clerical home in the Cathedral city of Rochester. The barrier, once broken, collapsed. It had been a stiff one. What would the outcry of the Rev. Patrick Brontë have been if his 'difficult' daughter Emily, whom one surmises might have become as dominant and frightening a tragedienne as Sarah Siddons, had bolted from the moorland rectory at Haworth to join a troupe of players on the Yorkshire circuit?

The Shakespearian actors in relation to the Patrons had a position similar to that of the between-stairs Victorian governess. The Sonnets reveal the curious mixture of close friendship with a nobleman with a sense of inferiority; the actor was attached to a great house, but he was there by favour, a servant but not one of the menials. A domestic staff has its own snobbery and keen sense of grading. (On a liner I have heard a cabin-steward say that his Christmas dinner had been ruined by his having to sit next to a bath-steward.) It is likely that the fetchers and carriers and washers-up took a very poor view of actors at large in the mansion and taking wine with his lordship.

The players' society was localised. Its members lived close to the theatres in Shoreditch and Southwark. They took their recruits from those whose ambitions and aptitudes drew them in, with approval, if justified, to follow. It was largely a family business, with apprentices observing the romantic tradition and marrying the master's daughter. Shakespeare brought in his short-lived brother Edmund who was buried, at more than usual cost, in St Mary's at Southwark. That was their parish and their 'patch'.

Ben Jonson was buried in Westminster Abbey in 1637 when he had long ceased to be an actor and had become a prominent literary lion. To the Abbey, too, went Francis Beaumont, the son of a knight, playwright not player. On the whole the profession knew its place on the fringe of the Court and in the heart of the play-going commoners. The phrase 'sitting snug' is sometimes used in the theatre of one who has had the sense to secure his future. The King's Men became middle-class citizens with middle-sized prosperity. They were snug enough.

In a lawsuit of 1619 Heminge was described as a man of 'great lyvinge wealth and power'. That need not be taken as a proof of imposing opulence. He was the defendant in a dispute about the alienation of theatre shares left by Augustine Phillips. The plaintiff, John Witter, who had married Augustine's widow, would naturally like to present Heminge as a plutocrat. The quarrels about the tenure and sales of holdings recounted in the Sharers' Papers show that the actors and their families were vigilant guardians of their rights and did not mind the cost and trouble of going to law. When Shakespeare made Hamlet complain of 'the law's delay' he knew what he was talking about. 'Witter *versus* Heminge and Condell' came into court fourteen years after the death of Phillips.

Like the farmers and tradesmen of Stratford, whose zeal in suing one another made a good living for the local lawyers, the players in London, some occasionally battling with steel in the street, came to fight each other in litigation. That is a bourgeois, not a Bohemian, exercise. It is typical of men with a passion for possession, used to legal pleadings and papers. In the story of the Earl of Montgomery's career as Lord Chamberlain it was seen that he was involved in a similar contention about a sale of shares in the Globe and Blackfriars. These theatres had not been the gold-mines searched for by the explorers and 'projectors' of the period, but they had provided solid investment for solid, shrewd and tenacious men who expected to 'sit snug'.

The Victorian actors, like the Shakespearians, could make sufficient to save and retire. Squire Bancroft was able to stop acting at forty-four because he had persuaded the mid-Victorian public to pay ten shillings and sixpence for a stall to see him and his very popular wife, Marie Wilton, in successful comedies by Tom Robertson and others. In 1897 he followed Irving in the knighthood with less professional cause, but this was symptomatic of changing status. The Bancrofts had helped to put the actor on the map of High Society.

Before they began their upward progress the players' life was drawn in Sir Arthur Pinero's comedy *Trelawney of the Wells*. Half romantic and half realistic, it pictures early frustration leading to success amid a congenial mixture of true love and friendliness in cheap lodgings. The players are considered impossible company in a West End home. Contempt for the stage was countered by the career of William Macready, the eminent Shakespearian of the early Victorian theatre. He retired in 1851 to spend twenty years in comfortable retirement. In his youth he had wanted to be a barrister and was driven to the stage by lack of means to carry him through the early years at the bar. He enhanced the theatre's reputation not only by his fine presence, dignity, and splendid diction but by his participation in the literary society of his age. He was a close friend of Charles Dickens and his retirement evoked a salute from Tennyson, who had just become Poet Laureate. Had knighthoods then been admissible for esteemed stage-players he could well have anticipated the honour which came to Irving more than forty years later.

Since the arrival of the cinema and of broadcasting the financial scene has been entirely altered. The Mammoth Spectacular Film, sometimes with a text of Shakespeare's at the base of the monstrous creation, is capitalised in millions and can pay its stars accordingly. That is fair enough since without the crowd-compelling names the picture would not have been made at all. Thus Richard Burton and Elizabeth Taylor, who could not remain at the summit of reward if they did not earn it, can come happily to London with their yacht or anchor off Monte Carlo in the manner of a Greek Croesus. But, if they settled in England, it would be good-bye to all that since, following the last war and the vast expenditure on 'the public sector' of national finance, the taxation of vast incomes has become so vast as to make them meaningless.

The leading high-salary players who stay at home lose most of what they make and, if they are to get on with their work, have to employ the sharpest brains of the accountancy world to cope with the claims and keep what they can. Amid lucrative offers to fly here and there for television appearances as well as major roles in the lavishly financed films they are distracted people. To keep their heads amid the blaze and blare of publicity is a strain; to maintain their standard of work in this hurly-burly is a major achievement.

Tax avoidance, which is not tax evasion but the legitimate discovery and use of loop-holes in and ways round the law, has become a major necessity in the world of entertainment where Shakespearian players with star ranking are gilt-edged assets in company promotions. The actors who in their various media approach that valuation employ skilled professional advice while reasonably trying to rescue what they can from the grip of the Treasury. But a great artist should not be diverted by sharing in the taskwork of accountancy. One wonders what language Henslowe and Alleyn, Shakespeare and Heminge would have used if presented with an Income Tax Return and the ensuing demands. There is evidence that Shakespeare was at one time a tardy and reluctant payer of his petty local rates.

With a discreetly chosen foreign domicile and their box-office appeal maintained the stars can hold on to much of what they have earned by their gifts and by the experience gained in incessant work. Not all choose opulence involving exile. But this must not become an essay on financial strangulation. What is relevant is the effect of films and television on the players' way of life and on the quality of acting, especially in Shakespearian performance.

The prologues written for *Henry V* strongly suggest that the dramatist of the Globe's 'unworthy scaffold' would have welcomed, at least in prospect, the Mammoth Spectacular as filmed with a stupendous budget in the studios of Hollywood or 'on location' in Rome, Spain, or the Near East. He wanted a cavalry charge with horses 'printing their proud hoofs i' the receiving earth'. He could have had them by the hundred and he did in fact get a most impressive battle of Agincourt when Sir Laurence Olivier played in the film the rhetorical conqueror of that field. Amid the instruction usefully given in this memorable picture was the menace of martial archery in mass with its reminder that bows and arrows were not the weapons of sportive boys or park-land amateurs of the target. Shakespeare could have been

enraptured also by Sir Laurence's *Richard III*. *Hamlet* offered a
text too comprehensive for pictorial compression. The vast castle
loomed destructively over the text and the characters. What I
felt was needed was fewer of Elsinore's corridors and more
Shakespearian passages.

The fact that Shakespeare can be finely filmed in a manner
probably to his taste has been sufficiently proved despite some
absurd blunders of irrelevant display and mishandling of the text.
I remember the publicity boost I received before seeing an early
Hollywood 'picturization' of *Romeo and Juliet*. It included the
fantastic figures of expenditure and the number of livestock
assembled in herds. Apparently Verona was seen as a centre of
the wool and mutton trades. That was rash if counting sheep be
indeed an aid to sleep.

But the camera has given service of several kinds. A valuable
case of its employment was the straight photographic record made
of the stage production of *Othello* in which Sir Laurence as the
Moor was leading the National Theatre Company in London and
making the acquisition of a seat at the 'Old Vic' a test of patience
or a proof of privilege. Here on film was the play exactly as
performed with no fussy enlargement of spectacle, no Venice in
all its glory, no carnival of songful gondoliers, no storm at sea,
no 'travelogue' of Cyprus and its environs. If all the best-acted
and most admired stage productions of Shakespeare's plays
were thus preserved with no cinematic trimmings they would be
precious possessions for future directors in the theatre and for
historians of the stage.

If we could see an original performance of an Elizabethan 'first
afternoon' we might and almost certainly would be sadly aston-
ished by its paucity of players, its inadequate preparation and the
consequent muddle and confusion. We have no documented
information about the number of productions offered in a year
by Shakespeare's company but, even with higher standards, they
cannot have been greatly different from the output of their rivals.
We have got Henslowe's detailed account of the doings of the
Admiral's Men. In eleven months between June, 1594, and May,

1595, they staged thirty-eight plays of which eighteen were new. Richard David, in his published lecture on *Shakespeare and the Actors*, decided—and nobody can dispute his judgment—that 'the Elizabethan companies accepted and maintained a programme that to anyone with experience of repertory must seem quite staggering'. He also reminds us that the 'gatherers' who took the pence of the groundlings and the further pence of those buying seats in the galleries were enlisted as 'supers' for military and civilian crowd-work in order to increase the meagre number of the Hired Men. That must have been done when the play had started.

This was the practice at the Hope Theatre, built for Henslowe in 1613, when theatrical methods had outgrown their early crudity. Yet there, we are told, at least nineteen of the front-of-the-house staff were mustered to join the players. We are not told where and how much they changed their costumes and how much they had been given of even shadowy rehearsal. In the tiring-room, whose size we do not know, and on the stage the probability of chaos is obvious. Apparently Shakespeare's army at Agincourt, if it were, as he grumbled, but five or six, was not assisted by an influx of gatherers, but either way the production must have been pitiful by modern standards. Shakespeare's films have gone to the other extreme.

In some a colossal mob, well manipulated for clever camera-shots, was turned into a major attraction, dwarfing the individual players. A television studio cannot contain an army of cinematic size, but the temptation to play up the crowd in this medium can be disastrous. After a B.B.C. production of *Julius Caesar* it was complained by several critics, with whom I agreed, that the director was so anxious for the audience to lend him their eyes that Antony's request for their ears was frustrated.

There is a fundamental contradiction in the demands of cinema and stage where Shakespeare is concerned. That he would have liked spectacular drama he frankly stated; that he could not have it he knew and accepted. Therefore he used, with consummate ability, his only implement, the newly enriched and expanding English language written by himself and spoken by the players.

He was one of these, knowing that he had a mixed and sometimes restless and noisy audience to control. Fortunately it was a word-loving public at a time of verbal invention and a music-loving public with an ear for the cadence of a poet's phrase as well as for a boy's treble voice and the harmonies which the composers could provide. We have the words and some of the melodies. With good direction we can have authentic Shakespeare now, not exactly as his listeners had it then, but near enough to feel the strength and the sweetness and to appreciate the sounds which had to compete with the clatter and cheers in the Bear Garden next door. Rarely can savage and civilised entertainment have been closer neighbours in one way or more separated in another. In the early theatres, half open to the sky and the impact of the English climate, there had to be attack. Henry V's speech outside Harfleur is as apposite to the players as the troops.

Shakespeare, as was earlier pointed out, had several things to say about the troubles and handicaps of the actors. They sometimes failed to remember their lines and were 'beside the part'. The lesser men were conscious of a listless audience when the star had left the stage. They also felt themselves 'o'er-parted' in roles beyond their range. The tragedians strutted and some mistook bellowing for clear and forthright diction. But in none of his theatrical commentary does he mention the inaudibility which has become the curse of Shakespearian performance today.

That nuisance has partly been created by the cult of naturalism in the production of modern plays. It is assumed that because people mutter in their conversation stage-dialogue can be slurred in order to seem realistic. It is a matter of pride in a player of light comedy to score his points without emphasis. He is suspicious of 'a punch-line'. He believes and, if he is extremely skilled, he can sometimes prove that to 'throw away' a line gives it point because a lowered voice seems plausible and in character. Occasionally that comes off, but usually far more is lost than gained. Realism in handling a theme or drawing a character is fully justified. To carry it into conversation is vexatious. It is also illogical. The theatre is an artificial creation and its practice must be governed accordingly. The tributes to Burbage praised the compelling realism of the emotions which he portrayed. He could not have held an audience if he had talked on the stage as he did to a friend over a glass in a tavern.

The major cause of natural speech on the stage has been the invention of the microphone. That device is excellent for producing the effect of easy conversation. The statesman, now increasingly dependent on the television 'image' which he and his advisers in publicity create, must seem a friendly, fireside companion. He does not address the nation; he talks to it. The old political rhetoric is completely outdated. There is no longer an art of eloquence. Sir Winston Churchill was the last of the political orators. Before him Franklin Roosevelt's use of sound radio had established the conversational manner of winning the ear of his people. The eye-to-eye photographic image and the heart-to-heart 'chat up' have prevailed. The politician is an actor who seeks to seem the quiet man confiding his opinions and not a spokesman announcing and denouncing. The microphone is itself a confidence trick and the politicians who use it most effectively are 'con men'.

The actors for film and television cannot be rhetoricians. If they tried to be they would jam the machinery. To be outspoken is to put 'a spanner in the works' of a recording studio. Speech must be muted and movement limited to the space available. The production of a televised feature or play with little rehearsal time to spare (and usually there is no chance for long consideration) has seemed to me, as I watched it, a miracle of co-operating contrivance. The number of technicians is many and their ability remarkable. They work under the direction of a man who is thinking of necessity as much in terms of visual effect as of verbal meaning. Big films, with their larger budgets and more elastic time-tables, admit of more corrections and re-takes. But where there is a camera it is master of the operations. Plays and players are fed into a machine and their words frequently seem to matter less than their appearance.

The leading players of today have been described as distracted.

Heavy demands on their stamina are made and met. Burbage had to slog on with the study of a new and demanding part while another occupied his afternoons. He was not living at the end of a telephone or dashing to an aerodrome. Nor did he have to cope with new inventions and modulate his voice to a microphone.

Now there are diverse and far-flung invitations involving fast and frequent travel which can be most exhausting. (As I write this Sir Laurence Olivier has just been jet-propelled to and fro across the Atlantic within twenty-four hours while playing a major role at the 'Old Vic' where he had the burden of the chief command.) Those who are not so much on the wing are often engaged in studios by day while working in London theatres at night with two performances on Saturdays. That is more than a physical and nervous strain. It means adapting their methods of playing to the cameras for twice as many hours in a day as they are facing a live audience.

This can be done. The seniors have abundantly proved their capacity for such a change-over. Sir John Gielgud stays mainly on the stage but he is also as superb an exponent as Sir Laurence of Shakespearian acting on the screen. His voice, with its perfect conveyance of the meaning as well as the music of his lines, is accommodated to the microphone without loss of power when he returns from the studio. While playing Cassius to Marlon Brando's Antony in a film of *Julius Caesar* he convincingly exposed the difference between a stage-actor and a film star in roles written for the stage. This is not to denigrate a popular idol of the cinema public. It is merely to stress that an expert in one medium can be at a loss in the other. Brando was the specialist, Gielgud the dualist.

Sir Ralph Richardson is a further example of the ability to move with assurance and mastery from one world to the other. The new distractions do not diminish the effectiveness of experienced men and women. The Dames have proved as surefooted as the Sirs in their passage from stage to studio and back again. Those who knew how to alter and adjust their techniques are not hampered by their years. Dame Edith Evans received an

Oscar award for her film-work when she was eighty. Had she walked straight back into a theatre not a word of her part or a fraction of its meaning would have been lost. But the youngest generation, who seem to be inadequately schooled in voice-production, fall into gabbling in a supposedly realistic manner. Training in traditional elocution is now suspect as a cause of the forthright acting which is stupidly dismissed as 'ham' when the player is audible and is determined to attack.

The newcomers are in a difficult position. The profession is overcrowded and stage-parts are few compared with the opportunities offered by the cinema and especially by television whose plays and series of plays have to come streaming on to the air throughout the week on several channels. Here there are millions of viewers to be pleased, more scope for engagements, and larger rewards. Entry can be swift and reputation swiftly made if a lucky chance is well taken. Once it was almost obligatory in the theatre for a young recruit to learn his or her job on tour or in the hard grind of a minor repertory company. Now there is the strong temptation to hang on in the capital lest a precious telephone call from an agent be missed. For various reasons touring has dwindled while televised plays have multiplied and for them a microphone voice may be sufficient.

It is not surprising that, if a part in a Shakespeare production in a theatre does come along, it will discover the weakness of the player who has had more studio than stage experience. My recent attendance at a performance of *Love's Labour's Lost* showed that, while the men were at least adequate, the young women seemed to be bewildered and even bored by the words. They had been well rehearsed in graceful movement. They 'looked a picture'. This comedy is partly a dance of words and a touch of ballet in the direction is well justified. But the characters should know what they are talking about and make some show of caring for their meaning.

When film directors are devising a Shakespearian production in their own medium then there is bound to be more concentration on the picture than on the poetry. That is what most of their huge public want. An international market has to be won. If men with a film reputation are brought into the theatre they bring with them their natural addiction to the visual effect. To some of them English is a foreign language and Elizabethan English an additional puzzle. They may not even know the text. John Stride, who was an excellent young lover in Signor Zeffirelli's direction of *Romeo and Juliet* for the National Theatre Company, told an audience to whom he was talking about it that the director had explained to the players that the Montagus were aristocrats and the Capulets upstarts. Shakespeare had plainly told his audience in the very first line of the brief introductory Chorus speech that he is telling a tale of 'Two households both alike in dignity'. Nothing could be clearer. Nothing was gained by flatly contradicting the author.

The time-scheme of the Elizabethan theatre and the nature of the cuts which it demanded have been discussed in an early chapter. Their actors are known to have been trained in a formal style of elocution. They could not race through their speeches. It may be a tribute to Shakespeare that we cut less and are proud of presenting a full text. This can be given because the pace of acting has steadily risen. That has occurred to a marked extent in contemporary comedy which is taken at a gallop to put across three acts of light entertainment in less than two hours. Brief and brisk is the rule for a fashionable trifle.

The application of this speed to the classics which were written for a different style of projection has sometimes added to the confusion caused by muttered speaking. If the length is excessive it would be better to cut more and speak it better. One of the most lively and inventive directors of old plays, Sir Tyrone Guthrie, has whisked them along at the cost of the words. He manœuvres his team with a most engaging freshness, but he encourages a kind of gabble which would have dismayed the actors of the past and would have shocked Shakespeare. Hamlet criticised slow mouthing and wanted speech to flow 'trippingly on the tongue'. But, he added, if the passion of the part was tempestuous, the acting was to have 'a temperance that may give

it smoothness'. Smooth speech is lucid and lucidity is swamped
in a torrent unless the player is exceptionally gifted.

It is inevitable that well-thumbed classics such as Shakespeare's
plays should be handled by new fingers tingling with the excitement of a challenge. The innovator feels that he must prove his
quality by offering a fresh interpretation or providing a new look.
There have been many fanciful changes of period and costumes.
Those theorists who dote on long words have proclaimed their
portentous '-isms'. I have seen a production of *Hamlet* amid a
mass of packing-cases announced as an essay in Constructivism.
On open stages, apron stages, and platforms of other kinds
Expressionism has jostled Surrealism. When a fashionable director told me that he was intending an Existentialist version I asked
him to explain what he meant. He could not do so and was merely
using the jargon of the artistic intellectuals. It is understandable
that the *'avant garde'* should want to escape from routine. It is
desirable that they should understand what they are talking about
when they are giving interviews and making pronouncements
about their plans and policies.

It is a fair conclusion that the director of a play should realise
as closely as possible the author's intention and not put forward
his own ideas of what he thinks the author meant to say or should
have said better. If it is a piece of today the dramatist may speak
for himself if he is not overborne by a manager and director
convinced of his own superior wisdom. That does happen. In the
case of Shakespeare there is inevitable doubt and dispute about
the purpose and emotional background of a play. But his wishes
about the performance and mounting of a play were publicly
stated in the prologues for *Henry V* and in Hamlet's talks to the
players.

He would have liked more spectacle, larger resources and more
manpower. Therefore he could have been excited and delighted
by the idea of a play sumptuously made into a Super-Film. The
result he might have rejected as false to his thinking, but the
previous prospect of some benefit to the eye would have been
alluring. He might, too, have welcomed the massive crowds and

canvas which a Victorian and Edwardian actor-manager could finance. Shaw castigated Irving for putting the scenery, monstrous or magnificent according to taste, before the scripts which were abbreviated and adjusted to the amount of painting and carpentry enjoyed by their public. But we must remember, before we scold, that Shakespeare made no effort to preserve the texts of his plays. There is no evidence that the very personal Sonnets were published with his permission. Sensible trimming of the plays' great tapestry of words is no crime. Hamlet had said of too long a speech, 'It shall to the barber's.' He did not regard cutting as an insult to the author. From the actors he demanded truth to nature in presenting a character. He wanted fluency of speech in a strong but not feverish or turbulent display of high emotion. There was to be rhetoric without rant.

In my period of intense admiration for Granville-Barker's production of Shakespeare I agreed with his provision of a full text, but I am not so sure of that now. To insist on every word is a form of loyalty to the Bard. It is not necessarily in accord with the practice of his time and team.

A recent experience of Shakespearian acting in London was Hamlet played by a man recently praised with good cause for his vigour in contemporary work, a man of impressive power. He knocked royalty out of the Prince and poetry out of the part. He rattled the role along like a jolting vehicle on a rough road. The whirligig of time sets theatrical fashion spinning. Some deliberately advocate the playing down of Shakespearian kings and noblemen. They must be drab folk, to suit the age of the common man. We must not be snobs. We must not be smooth. Rudeness is all, not quite all, perhaps, but toughness is the trend. Bad temper is better acted than good looks are displayed.

If I end with praise of senior or departed players I am not assuming that they will have no equals. There is a young entry of high promise in the subsidised companies which alone can now afford Shakespearian production. The important thing is that they should not be too much distracted by those offers from other sources which their talents naturally evoke. That way lies another type of performance, a far larger public and the chance of a diminished ability to take a stage and hold an audience.

C. E. Montague said of Sir Johnston Forbes-Robertson's Hamlet that 'the beauty of each gesture and tone was almost abstract in its purity'. Beauty has now become an ugly word in the arts, but there was nothing sentimentally moist or mawkish in the beauty of many Shakespearian performances in my time. John Barrymore's Hamlet with Fay Compton's Ophelia marked a summit of visual and aural appeal. Vivien Leigh's Cleopatra shimmered on the heights where the eye dazzles. Henry Ainley had a presence and a voice to make gods of earthbound men. Perhaps he bothered less than the others about the meaning of his lines but he sent them soaring. He may not have known what Hamlet was talking about, but how he talked! Godfrey Tearle, Ainley's Horatio, gave that part its true importance and spoke to perfection. He touched nothing of Shakespeare's which he did not decorate.

Sir John Gielgud, whose musical delivery is so finely varied and so well married to the text, was a complete actor at twenty-five. At that age he and Ralph Richardson, then twenty-seven, both in the emerging phase and a long way from titled eminence, took the leads in two long series of Shakespearian productions at the 'Old Vic'. The intervals between them were only three weeks. They were as hustled as the Chamberlain's Men. That was no hindrance to performances which were as able as ambitious. The results were unforgettable for those who were there. I think that the master dramatist would have been glad to meet these young masters in the making.

He would have been delighted too by the shrill drollery of Sir Laurence Olivier's Justice Shallow, a brilliant contrast with the dynamic villainy of his Crookback and his driving penetration of the sad hearts of broken heroes. There have been, to use Thomas Hardy's title, 'a group of Noble Dames', Thorndike, Evans, Ashcroft, who would never blunt the wit or slur the pathos of a part. Since 1945 Paul Scofield has arrived as a worthy heir to a great succession.

I end with the memory of a man once thought to rank below the top class. The knighthoods have not been given without discrimination. Shortly before the far too early death of Sir Donald Wolfit I saw his compelling picture of Pastor Manders in an excellently televised rendering of Ibsen's *Ghosts*. There experience told. Once deemed too 'robustious', he could change his forceful methods on the stage to the delicacy of a camera performance. He had had to be robust, working for many years and in all sorts of theatres and to all sorts of audiences widely spread as did the original Elizabethan companies. He had been a dominant figure in all sorts of parts including the Marlovian Tamburlaine. One who is to move rapidly from Falstaff to Lear must take his characters as well as popular audiences by storm. No whispering. For that he was slighted by some as brash and booming. If he was that he grew out of it. A sour critic said of him that 'he should be acting in the middle of a field'.

Let us imagine Burbage with a new and enormous part in a new production. The bills have been posted. The gossip has gone round. The trumpets have sounded. The gatherers are still taking the pence of the Southwark groundlings and of the gentry who have been ferried over from the mansions and Inns of Court on the North Bank to sit in a half-open theatre amid the clatter of the South. The bright day has clouded. The wind comes roughly in from where a roof should have been. The audience, with some mannerless and even noisy elements, is as gusty as the weather. Here is rough country for the tenderness of the music and the poetry and for the long climb to the final poignancy of a tragedy. Out goes the voice and up the glory of the words. Was not Burbage 'acting in the middle of a field'?

Principal Books Consulted

✦

G. P. V. Akrigg, *Shakespeare and the Earl of Southampton*

T. W. Baldwin, *The Organization and Personnel of the Shakespeare Companies*

G. E. Bentley, *The Jacobean and Caroline Stage*

M. C. Bradbrook, *The Rise of the Common Player*

Oscar Campbell and Edward Quinn, *A Shakespeare Encyclopaedia*

Sir Edmund Chambers, *The Elizabethan Stage, William Shakespeare, Shakespeare Gleanings*

Margaret Chute, *Shakespeare of London*

W. Robertson Davies, *Shakespeare's Boy Actors*

E. I. Fripp, *Shakespeare, Man and Artist*

H. Granville-Barker, *Prefaces to Shakespeare*

F. E. Halliday, *A Shakespeare Companion, Shakespeare in his Age*

G. B. Harrison, *Shakespeare at Work*

Martin Holmes, *Shakespeare's Public*

G. L. Hosking, *The Life and Times of Edward Alleyn*

Leslie Hotson, *The First Night of Twelfth Night, Shakespeare's Sonnets Dated*

Elizabeth Jenkins, *Elizabeth the Great*

Sir Tresham Lever, *The Herberts of Wilton*

Peter Quennell, *Shakespeare*

M. M. Reese, *Shakespeare*

A. L. Rowse, *Shakespeare, Shakespeare's Southampton, Christopher Marlowe*

Irwin Smith, *Shakespeare and the Blackfriars Theatre*

A. C. Sprague, *Shakespeare and the Actors, Shakespeare's Audience, Samuel Daniel, Selected Works*

J. Dover Wilson, *The Essential Shakespeare, Shakespeare's Happy Comedies* and Introductions to the Cambridge University Press Editions of Shakespeare's Plays and Sonnets

Index